PLAYING GOD

PLAYING GOD

If You Could Be God, What Would You Do?

Dennis Edward Green

Boulevard Press

Copyright © 2013 Dennis Edward Green

All rights reserved. No part of this publication may be reproduced, distributed, or transmitted in any form or by any means, including photocopying, recording, or other electronic or mechanical methods, without the prior written permission of the publisher, except in the case of brief quotations embodied in critical reviews and certain other noncommercial uses permitted by copyright law. For permission requests, write to the publisher, addressed "Attention: Permissions Coordinator," at the address below.

This is a work of fiction. The names, characters, businesses, places, events and incidents are products of the author's imagination. Resemblance to actual persons, living or dead, or actual events is coincidental. I have tried to recreate events, locales and conversations from my memories of them. In order to maintain their anonymity in some instances I have changed the names of individuals and places, and I may have changed some identifying characteristics and details such as physical properties, occupations, and places of residence.

ISBN   978-0-9832411-7-1 Hardback
ISBN   978-0-9832411-5-7 Trade Paperback
ISBN   978-0-9832411-6-4 e-book

Library of Congress Catalog Number 2013901571

Publisher: Boulevard Press
80499 Spanish Bay
La Quinta, CA 92253
Editor: Mary Lou Green

http://www.BoulevardPress.com

Ordering Information:
Quantity sales. Special discounts are available on quantity purchases by corporations, associations, clubs, and others.
For details, contact: Sales@BoulevardPress.com.

To contact the author, go to:
http://www.DennisAndMaryLou.com

To Mary Lou—my wife, partner,
inspiration, guardian angel, editor, muse
and best friend

Acknowledgments

Special thanks to my dear friends: Patti Arnieri, Karla Hawley, Jan Gurney, and Brooklin Pesetski—for reading my early draft and offering valuable insights in shaping, refining, and editing my manuscript. I know I gave you a lot to do!

To my amazing friends: Bob & Felice Nelson, Joe and Joan Garrett, Jim Fleming, Xavier Zamarripa, Tom Wiener, Barbara Humphrys, Dan Rulli, Mona Stephens, Claire and John Arnold, Patti Cooke, Kathleen Harkness, Dr. Ravi Rao, Nancy Franks, and Kae Hammond—thank you for taking time out of your busy lives to offer helpful ideas and encouragement.

Deep gratitude to Charles and Hilary St. John—I so appreciate your wise counsel and sincere, pull-no-punches comments. I miss our weekly movie and dinner nights where we could talk about these ideas on end.

I especially want to thank my family for their lifelong support: my talented son, Dennis, who guides me even when he doesn't know it, and my brilliant daughter-in-law, Kathleen, who appreciates my droll humor; my thoughtful and enthusiastic brother, Patrick, and his gorgeous and accomplished wife, Teri, who accept me for who I am; and my beautiful and witty sister, Sharon Ridgway, the best writer in the family. Also a special thanks to my mother-in-law, Mary Ann Wickens, for being the best cheerleader on the planet. All of you have encouraged me to do my best and forgiven me when I didn't write or call as often as I should.

Finally, Mary Lou, thanks to your left brain for editing this book with unflagging energy at every stage, and to your right brain for providing the insights for me to step outside my box. Your unfailing belief in me is priceless.

Table of Contents

In The Beginning — 13
"Changing the world felt impossible. Changing my thinking was a different story. In fact it turned out to be twenty different stories."

1. A Taste of Heaven — 21
He said, "Don't you think we'd all be more considerate of each other if we knew for sure what was waiting when we passed on?"

2. Innocent Cries — 25
"Behind your question is an assumption that I could be God. To assume that is terribly arrogant, wouldn't you say?"

3. Deserving Souls — 29
"He had me worried when he used the words 'rightsize' and 'targeted.' I urged him to continue even though his bizarre ideas made me uneasy."

4. The Less Impossible — 37
"Children learn too many useless facts, often simply because facts can be tested. We must stop teaching to the tests and stop testing the irrelevant."

5. Meaning of Survival — 45
"You don't just wheel up to the SS office and put your hand out. The money comes from somewhere out there in the electrosphere."

6. Autograph Please — 53
"God?" he said. "How could I be God? That's weird. What kinda question is that?"

7. Unconditional   57
"When you came into the store and asked me what I would do if I could be God, I thought about how much I'd give to redo the last two years."

8. BDO   63
"If I could be God," he started in again, "I would give everyone a BDO."

9. The Producer   67
"Now if I could make Iron Man into a relationship picture—everybody in the business would think I was God."

10. Discovery   71
"It doesn't hurt me, so why should I mind? I love him. He's a great guy." She paused and smiled again. It was a wry smile. "But it is funny to watch."

11. Don't You Think?   77
"God gave us free will," she said. "We are the ones who can screw up this world or make it better."

12. All You Need to Know   83
"God is a concept, and that concept is very personal and different for everyone. It explains why we have thousands of different religions in the world."

13. Who Cares?   91
"During the entire time with her, I felt like a tea kettle with the top glued on, ready to blow. I resented feeling that I was being taken for granted."

14. In This Together   99
"When we say anyone can succeed if they work hard enough—it's all relative. How often do you hear a poor person say anyone can succeed?"

15. Now What's Wrong?   111
"I have been shopping at Ralphs for years, ever since they set up their club program, so why didn't my number work?"

16. Secrets   117
"Of course God has a point of view. Why else do you think he made humans? He likes to watch us fall crazy in love."

17. Miss Direction   125
"Ben looked like he was about to tackle her as she pranced off like one of those Victoria's Secret Angels. But she was no angel."

18. Ascot & Red   131
Red said, *"He's not asking you, Satan. He wants to know what a normal person would do if she could be God."*

19. The Emancipator   135
"It takes courage to quit some things. So get out there and quit what isn't working. Then go fail at something. It will give you courage."

20. The Atheist   143
She stopped for a moment then she said, *"I don't need to be saved. I need to feel loved."*

Author's Notes   155
"If you start dreaming above the clouds, you will have a lot more choices about where to stop on your way down to earth."

About the Author   164
Husband, father, and grandfather. He is also an award-winning architect, artist, graphic designer, entrepreneur, and best-selling author.

In The Beginning

"Changing the world felt impossible. Changing my own thinking was a different story. In fact it turned out to be twenty different stories."

One evening my wife and I saw a movie that made me think about God. It was not a religious movie. In fact it was a violent movie filled with murder and mayhem in a future world gone mad. The film wasn't the only thing that elevated my thoughts about God that day. On the way to the theater, we heard on the car radio about a two-year-old girl who drowned in the family's backyard swimming pool. Another story described a multiple-victim killing in Sweden.

Every day we learn about earthquakes, hurricanes, or tornadoes that decimate towns and villages and kill hundreds, even thousands, of people. It is hard to understand why we have so much death and destruction in our world.

People say they don't understand how God can let these terrible things happen. I understand that feeling, yet I know that God has nothing to do with our problems. God doesn't cause earthquakes, or car crashes, or any of the crazy stuff that humans can dream up to hurt one another. Still, that doesn't preclude me from wanting someone to take charge and intercede to stop the insanity that we see all around us. I wanted to do something to make life feel more hopeful. That night, after the movie, I felt this need in an exceptionally strong way.

After the movie, Mary Lou and I stopped at a little pizza place in Palm Desert and talked about the film. I told her how it affected me. She shared my feelings; then she asked the question that led to this book.

"I know you believe that God doesn't meddle in our lives or perform miracles," she said, "but what if *you* could? What if *you* could be God? What would you do?"

I thought for a moment. It was an intriguing idea.

"I'm serious, what would you do?" she said.

"Well I guess for starters, I would work on the major problems like war, disease, hunger, poverty, and hatred. What about you? What would you do?"

"I'd start with the things you mentioned. Then I would clean up the environment and deal with climate change. I would also work on some personal things."

"Such as?"

"Self-esteem, for one. I'd give everyone the confidence to succeed and feel good about themselves."

We went back and forth like that for awhile, then Mary Lou suggested I ask our waiter, a young Latino with a happy smile, what he would do if he could play God. When he came around to our table, I said to him, "Can I ask you a question?"

"Certainly. Can I get you something?"

"I would like to know what you would do if you could be

God."

"I'm sorry?" he said, with a blank look, like he was trying to fathom my question.

I repeated, "If you could play God, what would you do to make the world a better place or change something to improve your personal life?"

He grinned nervously. "What do you mean?"

I asked the question one more time.

Finally, he said, "Do you mean what would I change . . . if I could be God . . . you mean God, God?"

"Yes, God, God."

He glanced up toward the ceiling, thinking. He sighed and said, "I don't know, maybe I would give all the poor people some money."

I was curious. "How much money?"

"I don't know," he said, "a lot, I think." Then he added, "That is a really interesting question." And he walked away, his eyes scrunched up like he was thinking, why do I always get the weirdos?

Mary Lou and I talked about his answer. What if all of the poor people in the world suddenly became rich? A few minutes later the waiter returned to our table.

"One million dollars," he said. "I would give each poor person one million."

Soon, another waiter, a young woman with ash-blonde, straight hair came by the table. I guessed she was about twenty-five. She said, "I wouldn't change anything."

Obviously our waiter had shared my question. "Really?" I asked. "Why not?"

"Because the world is too complicated. Once you change one thing, you can't predict what will happen because of it."

"Is it important for you to predict the outcome of every change? You can't predict the future now, so why does it matter?"

"You can't play God with the world. Nobody is smart enough. Look at the lottery winners. A lot of them say they were happier before they had so much money." I assumed she was referring to the other waiter's idea.

While we were eating, the male waiter kept walking by and smiling, like he was pleased with his decision. We talked more about this idea of playing God; then we finished and went home.

That night I stayed awake thinking about what it would mean to be God, to have the power to do anything. Most of the ideas Mary Lou and I kicked around at the restaurant were big ideas, pie in the sky. I didn't have any delusions about suddenly waving a wand and ending war or curing cancer. So what was the point of thinking I could be God? The exercise was interesting, but I wasn't sure how it would make a difference.

About three in the morning, I suddenly realized that I was looking at the wrong problem. Mary Lou and I had been in business for many years. We invented consumer products together, and we learned the hard way about overextending ourselves. We had a lot of big ideas, but we didn't always have the resources or the technical knowledge to turn them into viable products.

Now I was doing the same thing with this idea. I was tackling all of the world's problems at once instead of focusing closer to home on something I had the power to change, something within my sphere of influence. Changing the world can feel impossible. Changing my own thinking is a different story. In fact it turned out to be twenty different stories.

The next morning we were sitting on the couch having coffee, and I told Mary Lou that I had a plan for how I was going to change the world. I told her I wanted to write a collection of stories about what people said they would do if they could play God. It would be a book focused on the sort of personal problems that people can solve by imagining they are God.

"How will this change the world?" she asked

"I remember something that Mother Teresa said, 'Not all of us can do great things, but we can all do small things with great love.' I believe that we can change the world by making small positive changes in ourselves. That will be the purpose of this book. I'll start by asking people what they would do if they had absolute power to change anything in their lives. Then I will evaluate the responses and use the best stories to inspire more people to unleash their imaginations and change their own lives in positive ways. The small, positive changes that each of us makes will change the world for the better."

"Is this like asking, 'What would Jesus do?'"

"Not exactly. That question made us consider our values. I want my question to stimulate our imaginations, to help us see possibilities for change. Playing God is provocative, like asking, what if …?"

"You want to provoke me to think outside the box?"

"Not exactly that either. This is about motivating you to

step outside your box, so you can see yourself from all sides. Playing God takes you outside of yourself. It lets you look back at yourself from an objective point of view. You can see your problems as if they belong to someone else. And we know how easy it is to tell others how to solve their problems."

"Okay. So the stories will be the catalysts to start me thinking about how to address my own problems."

"Yes. The stories will show how other people crossed their mental boundaries—how they stepped outside their boxes, unleashed their imaginations, and changed their lives—all by imagining they could be God."

"It sounds very interesting. I can't wait to see what kind of answers this question sparks. When will you begin this quest?"

"This afternoon."

A few hours later I began asking friends and acquaintances at our health club what they would do if they could play God. I wasn't surprised to hear that virtually everyone was passionate about curing cancer and other diseases. They also wanted to end starvation, prevent wars, clean up the environment, even fix potholes in the streets. But I worried that if I kept hearing the same ideas over and over, my book would be very short and not much of a catalyst.

Then a conversation with a young woman who worked there pointed me in a new direction. After she identified the usual problems, I asked if there was *anything else* she would do perhaps to change her personal life. With my urging she confessed that, if she could play God, she would send her manager to Hell for how he treated the employees.

That was a surprise. Revenge was not the kind of good idea I had in mind. But it showed me something. From that day on, when anyone finished telling me the usual things they hoped to do, I asked if there was anything else. This book is a collection of the fascinating answers that fit the *anything else* category.

Each story was inspired by an actual conversation, situation, or person. I structured each interview and conversation to make it readable and provide a beginning, middle, and end to the story. For that reason, I consider this to be a work of fiction even though you would find it in the **self-help/creativity/motivation** section of the bookstore.

In many cases, I hungered to know more about the characters I met, but not knowing them was something I had to accept, as I knew many of them only briefly in passing.

Please come to our website, and let us know how you feel about the stories and the characters. I'm curious about your favorites, and whether you want to read more about them. When you come to our website, be sure to click on the **Contact** button, so we can get back to you. Here is the address:

htttp://www.DennisAndMaryLou.com

I hope these characters inspire you to write your own story as a way of unleashing your imagination and changing your life. The next time you are with a friend, ask them what they would do if they could play God. Their answer will surprise you.

—Dennis

A Taste of Heaven

He said, "Don't you think we'd all be more considerate of each other if we knew for sure what was waiting when we passed on?"

At first it wasn't easy for me to walk up to a stranger and ask what they would do about the world if they could play God. But some of the most interesting answers came from people I didn't know at all. I will give you an example.

While standing on a street corner one afternoon, waiting for the light to turn green, I noticed a guy about twenty yards away standing by the side of the road holding a sign. I couldn't make out what was written on the sign, but the fact that he was dressed in clean casual clothes, like an office worker, piqued my curiosity. I watched him walk away from the curb and settle down on the grass in the shade of a big tree—one of God's better ideas.

Perhaps he was a campaign worker, or maybe advertising something. I decided to investigate. As I approached, I noticed that his eyes were closed like he was enjoying a break. The sign lay flat on the ground beside him. In bold print it read, "Will Work For Free." Now that grabbed my attention.

You don't expect to see someone dressed like him standing by the side of the road holding a sign, let alone advertising that he is willing to work for nothing.

He opened one eye and offered a tentative smile. I introduced myself. He told me his name was Kevin. I guessed he was about forty-five. We chatted for a few minutes, then I asked him about the way he was dressed and about his sign. I told him I'd never seen anything like that.

"You know," he said, "I have not been able to find a regular job. I sent out resumés, made calls to friends—all the usual things." He sighed and shook his head at the futility. "I got nothing. But I want to work, so here I am. I think people are more willing to trust me if they think I'm dressed for work. By the way, you're standing in my conference room." He laughed.

I smiled. "What about your offer to work for free? How can you make money giving away your time?"

"Reciprocation."

"What does that mean?"

"If somebody gives you something, you feel obligated to give back. When I give freely, people naturally feel like returning the favor. I don't ask for money, but ninety percent of the time people pay me anyway, and usually more than I might have charged. People always need help with something. Then they see me standing here with my sign, and they pull around the corner into the parking lot. They want to know if I can help them move a bed, or cut down a tree, or solve a problem with their computer. That's my speciality and why I wear this." He pointed to his baseball hat with the word *Geek* boldly printed on the front panel.

"One thing leads to another. I come back to this corner when I'm not helping somebody. A lot of traffic passes this intersection. Word of mouth. I'm the guy on this corner that can do just about anything you need."

He told me about a few of his strange jobs. Then I told him I was writing a book and explained the premise. I asked him what he might do if he could be God. He didn't answer right away. He closed his eyes again and leaned back against the tree, like he was giving my question serious consideration.

After a long pause, he said, "You know what I've always wanted to do?"

"What?"

"I'd like to fence off the whole Mojave Desert, right here in California, turn it green, and create a model of Heaven on earth—like the Garden of Eden. Then I'd give everybody a chance to try it out."

"Try it out?"

"We think Heaven is this wonderful place, a paradise. But we don't really know, do we? Why not create somewhere to go so you can see for yourself? I used to be in real estate. Before the recession, my thing was building model homes. Model homes sell houses, you know."

"I'm sure. Are you saying you think people would live better lives if they could get a taste of Heaven now?"

"Precisely. I think we'd all be more considerate of each other if we knew for sure what was waiting when we passed on. That is our greatest fear, isn't it? We don't know what happens when we die. A model Heaven would clear that up."

I was knocked out by this idea. Wacky, but fascinating!

"How long would they get to tour your model Heaven?"

"Three weeks, and I'll tell you why. When I was a builder, I worked seven days a week. My wife was always trying to get me to take her on a vacation, a real vacation. She wanted three weeks. Finally, we saved enough. Things were a little slow, so we went to Hawaii. We had a marvelous time. It really is paradise. We could build a model of Heaven there, but it's a little far to go for most people on the mainland. Here's my point about three weeks. The first week I was wound up like a Swiss watch, worried all the time that if my developers needed something, they would go to one of my competitors. Then the second week I started to relax. By the end of week three, I didn't want to go home. That's why I think three weeks is about the right amount of time. It would really sink in that Heaven is worth waiting for."

"How would people find out about it?"

"I don't know." He thought for a few moments. "Maybe I'd start out with a little ad on Craigslist that said, 'Visit Heaven Now.'" He sat there for a moment, almost in a trance, then he looked up and point at the sky and shouted, "Yes!"

He jumped to his feet, brushed off his pants, and said he had to run. "Thank you, thank you!" Then he shook my hand.

"What are you thanking me for?" I said.

"You gave me a great idea, and I'd love to continue our conversation, but I gotta go."

"What about all of your potential customers?"

"They can wait. Right now I need to get to my computer. I can have the website built by Friday."

"What website?"

He grinned and said, "VisitHeavenNow.com."

Innocent Cries

"Behind your question is an assumption that I could be God. To assume that is terribly arrogant, wouldn't you say?"

Los Angeles to New York is a five-hour flight. Unfortunately, I was shoehorned into the middle seat. A nun sat in the aisle seat on my right. When I saw a young mother coming down the aisle with a baby in her arms, I knew she was destined for the window seat next to me. How did I know this? Because that's the way it works when you are six-foot-four and hoping for a nap.

Her baby was an angel now, but I knew when the air pressure in his little sinus cavities changed at takeoff, he would complain the only way he knew how. The fact that this was a long, nonstop flight had me on edge.

Once she settled in, the young mother smiled at me and introduced herself as Trish. Her baby's name was Jake. She was originally from New Jersey, and they were flying back there to be with her family for Jake's baptism. She said her husband was in the Marines and had recently deployed—she said she wasn't supposed to say where. They had been stationed near Palm

Springs, California, at the Marine Corps Air Ground Combat Center (also known as Twentynine Palms).

We took off, and sure enough, Jake woke up and began to protest the pain inside his head. They were innocent cries, so I didn't take them personally. Fortunately, I had just read Dina Proctor's book, *Madly Chasing Peace*, showing how three-minute meditations can counteract stress.

An hour into the flight, Jake was still crying. I was on the verge of a few tears myself. Trish looked like she hadn't slept since her husband deployed. I remember what sleep deprivation was like years ago when my son was colicky. I was in college, and there were times when I wanted to jump out the window and end it all, but as the old joke goes, it's hard to commit suicide leaping out of a basement.

Don't get me wrong, I love babies, and my son, but Jake had the lungs of a tuba player. I think every parent fears that their crying child might get them thrown off the plane, or even banned from flying by the International Airline Passengers Association. (Of course, I'm kidding. What are they going to do, stop the plane in Kansas City and ask them to leave?)

I noticed Trish rise in her seat, look toward the front of the plane, then to the back. I guessed she needed to use the lavatory and wondered what to do with Jake. It is hard enough to walk the center aisle of a plane dragging a rolling bag, but toting Jake and maneuvering inside an airplane lavatory would require Wonder Woman powers. I am certain I couldn't accomplish it. I think Trish was not looking forward to the challenge either.

She looked at me, her eyes shining like distress beacons. The nun was asleep. I was her only option.

"Let me take him for you, Trish," I said, feeling good about myself.

Her face brightened. At that point I don't think she cared if I was a serial killer. She needed out! I woke the nun, apologized for disturbing her, and told her I needed to stand so I could hold Jake while his mom visited the lavatory.

I stood in the aisle swaying with Jake and returning all of the sweet smiles I was getting from other passengers. It's nice to feel like a hero.

Trish returned, and we all settled back in our seats. She looked pleasantly surprised to hear that Energizer Jake had gone to sleep. I doubt it was anything I did. He was probably exhausted from an hour of pleading for relief from the pain caused by the air pressure change.

I told Trish to take a nap, and I would hold Jake for awhile. I mentioned I had a granddaughter to assure her I had the chops to handle whatever came along.

"Are you sure you don't mind?"

"Everything will be fine. You get some sleep." To be honest, I was enjoying the silence. I noticed her reach down to retrieve her purse. She took out a rosary made of hand-carved, wooden beads. She rested her head to one side and closed her eyes. I watched her fingers work on the rosary and imagined she was praying for her husband's safety—or maybe some sleep. A few minutes later her fingers stopped moving.

The nun said, "That was nice, taking the child."

"Self-defense," I replied, softly. "His name is Jake."

The nun nodded and smiled. "I heard you say that you have a granddaughter."

"Yes."

"I sometimes wish I were married and had children."

That was a surprise. No way could she mistake me for a priest, but I swear I had just heard a confession. It wasn't long before we were talking like old friends. Her name was Sister Mary Ignatius. I wondered how many nuns took that name. She had just returned from Guatemala where she was ministering to a tribe of Mayan Indians in the western highlands. She had been assisting a group of Catholic doctors and dentists who had traveled there to help the locals with various health problems. Her role was to convince mothers to let the doctors treat their children. She had been involved in this capacity for three decades.

Awhile into our conversation, she said to me, "And what keeps you awake most days?"

"Excuse me?"

"What is your purpose in life?" she said.

I must admit my purpose felt rather less important compared to hers. I told her a little about myself and eventually mentioned the book I was writing. I asked her, "If you could be God, is there anything else you would you do?"

"About what?"

"Anything. Your life. Airline food. Something to make the world a better place. If you had ultimate power, what more could you do for the children of Guatemala?"

"That is a strange question!" she said. "I am not sure it's appropriate."

"Excuse me?"

"Behind your question is an assumption that I could be

God. To assume that is terribly arrogant, wouldn't you say?"

"Not really. I think it's our responsibility to care for the planet. I don't expect God to solve our problems. It sounds like you don't either, based on your work in Guatemala. I'm just asking you to dream about the possibilities for improvement."

She stared into the seatback in front of her and sighed. "Well, yes, there are things I would change, but I wouldn't presume to be God."

"I understand. So what would you change if God gave you carte blanche? Imagine you had God's blessing to do anything."

"That's a smart rephrasing. Why are you asking me this question?"

"To unleash your imagination—so you can change your life or do something you never thought possible."

She didn't respond for a few moments, then she said, "As long as you put it that way, I will think about it."

A few minutes later she closed her eyes. I wondered if she was sleeping, or thinking about my question—or wishing she could move to another seat.

About halfway into the flight, everyone took their turns at the toilets again, then we all settled back in like chocolates in a Whitman's Sampler.®

About an hour passed when I heard Sister Mary say something that I couldn't understand. She was a small woman—the top of her head only reached to my shoulder—and the pilot was on the intercom sounding like a tour guide touting the Rocky Mountains visible out of the left side of the plane.

"Excuse me, Sister, what did you say?"

"You asked me what I would do if God granted me the

right to change the world, and now I am going to tell you what I would do."

"Okay, I'm listening."

"Good." She paused while the flight attendant passed by collecting garbage. "This is what I would do. I would sell all of the assets of the Church, including the Vatican, and I would create an endowment. It would be something like what Bill and Melinda Gates did, dedicated to eradicating diseases such as malaria and AIDS."

"You think that's possible?"

She looked at me with a disappointed frown. "If the Good Lord gives you the imagination to try something different," she said, "he has a very good reason, wouldn't you agree?"

"I can't argue with that."

She laid back against her headrest and looked up at the ceiling. "I know that the Pope will never sell the Vatican. It would never happen. But now you have me thinking."

"About what?" I asked.

"What if the Pope made the Vatican Bank extend micro loans to the poor to help them start small businesses and become self-sufficient by exporting their crafts all over the world?"

"Sounds like a plan to me."

"Fine," she said. "Can I count on your support?"

"What do you want me to do?"

"Talk about the possibilities in your book."

"I will. Is there anything else?"

"Yes. Pray that God will mention this to Pope Francis."

Deserving Souls

"He had me worried when he used the words 'rightsize' and 'targeted.' I urged him to continue even though his bizarre ideas made me uneasy."

Fundraising dinners are good for charities, which is why I attend them from time to time. The food and the conversation aren't usually very interesting, but this particular day was different, not because of the food, but because of the conversation I had with the guy sitting next to me. His name was Sandy. I'm guessing that he was about forty years old. He had worked on Wall Street until his company went bankrupt. He had moved to California about eight months ago to work for a hedge fund. He asked me what I did. I explained that I was writing a book about what people would do if they could play God. Eventually I got around to asking him what he would do if he had the ultimate power to change the world.

"What would I do if I could play God?" He frowned, sighed, then took a stalling sip of water. "What's the point?"

I wondered if he thought I was a religious nut. I doubted that a hedge fund manager would suggest giving money to the poor or financing a cure for cancer, but you never know. I shouldn't prejudge people; it's a nasty habit, like smoking.

I said, "The point is to unleash your imagination so you can do things you hadn't thought were possible. I believe that if you can let yourself dream the impossible, you can discover the less impossible, and that will help you achieve the possible."

He looked at me and blinked a few times. I got the feeling he was trying to decide if my premise was worth a response. Finally he said, "I would make the planet twice the current size. I mean, how are we going to support the fifty billion people that will be running around a century from now? Although maybe I shouldn't worry. Life on earth is like the stock market, ripe for a correction. No doubt we will accidentally create some sort of super virus that will reduce the population naturally."

If regret had a face, his nailed it. He had sad eyes. His thin upper lip curled into his mouth, forming a knife-blade line. I may have been reading too much into him because of the Wall Street thing, but he felt damaged and sounded bitter. I waited, sensing he had more to say.

"On second thought, why wait for nature to correct our numbers? If I were God, it would be easy to rightsize the population, starting now."

That gave me a start. "Rightsize?"

"I'd cut back on our numbers, not like in the Old Testament with a flood or a plague. I wouldn't be a one-size-fits-all kind of God. I wouldn't resort to natural disasters or viruses, either. I would be much more targeted."

"Targeted?" I was sitting there a bit stunned. Who was this guy?

"I would pick those souls that I knew would eventually dwell in the bottom of Dante's Nine Circles of Hell and target them for immediate punishment. This would include sociopaths, killers, liars, cheaters, and the worst of the greedy. Why wait? If I were God, I'd know who they are. I would be judge, jury, and executioner. Save society the expense. I wouldn't waste time letting them foul the planet and ruin the lives of good people. That would leave room for people who deserve to be here. Who knows? Maybe then we might survive with the planet in its present size."

He had me worried at the words "rightsize" and "targeted." I urged him to continue even though his bizarre ideas made me uneasy.

"For the virtuous, I would redesign the human body, which should have been done in the beginning. I would make our bodies more fuel-efficient, so we could consume fewer resources. I would also make us disease-resistant and heat-and-cold-resistant. Then I would deal with lifespan."

"Meaning?"

"Why do good people need to die? Some elements have a half-life of twenty thousand years. Why shouldn't humans who live a good life get to live forever? Aren't we more important than rocks or salt? If I could start from scratch, I would design life for better adaptation. If I could play God for just one hour—I don't need six days—I would eliminate all of the mistakes we have to live with, eliminate everything that doesn't work. I would clean up the planet to make it a paradise for the people who have earned the right to be here."

This guy was way out there. I wondered how his life experience affected his point of view. And I was curious about whether he was married or had kids. How did he sound around the house? He didn't seem to be what I would call a "fun guy." I asked him if he had a family. He looked uncomfortable with the question.

He took another slow drink of water and looked down and crumpled his napkin. He loosened his tie and unbuttoned his shirt. He wiped his mouth and cleared his throat. "As a matter of fact, my wife died a year ago. We didn't have any children."

"Oh, I'm sorry."

He waved it off, like he wasn't asking for sympathy. I didn't say any more. After a full minute of silence, he started talking about his wife.

"We were married for twelve years. She was an amazing woman. A beautiful person, inside and out."

"May I ask what happened to her?"

"Cancer of the blood cells...leukemia." His voice increased a notch. "There is no reason that should happen to such a wonderful person." He looked directly at me, his eyes intense and angry. "If we were properly designed in the first place, this would have been accounted for. Perfect blood shouldn't be hard to create—if you're God."

Before I could say anything, the master of ceremonies in the front of the room tapped the microphone and started making announcements. Sandy, the fund manager, stared at me; I should say he stared right through me. I had a feeling he was still thinking about his wife.

He looked away for a moment, then turned back to me and said, "How can we understand a world where the good die young, and the bastards live forever? Maybe your book can make sense of it. I sure can't—even if I were God."

At the front of the room, the speeches began, but I was still thinking about the look on his face. He was angry, but it wasn't a revenge anger, more like the hopeless kind, the kind that frustrates and depresses. The kind you feel when you lose the person you love most in the world and can't do a damn thing about it.

When the speeches were over, we got up to leave. He handed me his business card as we were walking out. I read the name of his hedge fund, which was innocuous enough. But beneath the company name, I saw something that surprised me. It also lifted my spirit and my estimation of this man for how he was dealing with his anger. It was a description of the company's purpose: *Funding Leukemia Research.*

He couldn't bring back his wife, but he seemed committed to doing something about the less impossible.

The Less Impossible

"At the present time, children learn too many useless facts, often simply because facts can be tested. We must stop teaching to the tests and stop testing the irrelevant."

A book publisher in Rancho Mirage invited us to a party for a friend of ours who had just written her memoir about growing up in the shadow of her movie star mother.

When we arrived, most of the people were outside. We saw our friend surrounded by well-wishers. I gave her a thumbs-up, and she waved back. It was midafternoon and the sun was bright; the temperature was a comfortable eighty degrees. We put on our sunglasses and went outside by the pool.

Mary Lou saw a woman she knew and excused herself while I roamed. I drifted over to a small group and listened to the conversation about the dire state of education in the public schools. I noticed one of the women wore the same style of sunglasses as mine—the kind with the leather cups on the sides to keep the sun from making wrinkles around your eyes. Not that I care about wrinkles, but I don't see many people wearing my style of glasses, so I felt a connection. In this Facebook era, I guess it doesn't take much to feel like a member of some tribe.

This woman's voice held incredible energy. One of the other women called her Andrea. She sounded confident and expressive, loaded with interesting ideas about how teaching and learning needed to change to keep up with evolving technology and social media. I eventually got around to joining the conversation. After we exchanged names, one person asked me if I was in publishing. I said I was an author working on a new book.

"What is your book about?" said Andrea with the cool sunglasses.

"It's about playing God."

"How do I do that?" she said.

"You play God by imagining that you are all-powerful and can do anything."

"I see," she said, emphasizing "see."

The other people laughed. I didn't understand why. It didn't sound funny to me. Anyway, I explained the premise. "When you play God, you are able to step outside your lifebox and see a world full of unlimited possibilities, ones that aren't apparent from sitting inside your box waiting for something to happen. Being all-powerful helps you imagine the impossible."

"What is the point of that?" asked the woman to Andrea's right. Her name was Jan.

"If we begin with the *possible*," I said, "we get what we've always had. If we start by imagining the *impossible* we stand a good chance of achieving what I call the *less impossible*. I like to believe that when we start dreaming above the clouds, we have a lot more choices about where to stop on our way down to earth. For example, Andrea, if you could be God, how would you change the world of education?"

"If I could be God?" She looked at me and tilted her head back with a laugh. "Oh, be careful what you ask for."

"This is your chance to fix everything that's wrong with education. No limits. What would you do?"

She smiled. "How much time do I have?"

"As much as you want. Tell me, what do you think is the greatest challenge to public education?"

"Money!"

"Money for what?"

"Unfunded health care liabilities for teachers and administrators. In California alone it is more than fifty billion dollars and rapidly growing, and it's going to demolish virtually every state budget over the next ten years. Few people will be able to afford a university education by then. The cost will be out of sight. Same with local elementary and high schools. School construction is another problem. We are already experiencing another baby boom, larger than the last. Where will these children go to school? Retired citizens, which will be the largest group by then, aren't going to keep issuing special school bond offerings forever."

"What's the solution?" I asked.

"The current approach is to cut costs and then cut some more. Cutting budgets is all people are talking about. But where does it end? When there are no more teachers? We have to be more creative in how we deliver and consume information and acquire knowledge."

"How would God solve this problem?"

"As God, I could add all cumulative knowledge to our

DNA. Life would be so much more exciting if we spent our time on the present and the future. If all knowledge were in our genes, like instincts, everyone would start life on an equal footing."

"What a wild idea!" Jan said. "Imagine newborns as smart as their parents!"

"Here's another idea," Andrea said. "I would give you a videographic memory so you would never forget ideas and information. If you had a video recorder in your brain, you would never miss a thing and could replay what you learned whenever you wanted. Best of all, your memories would be accurate."

Jan said, "That's definitely starting in the clouds. In reality, though, how do you get from the impossible to the less impossible?"

"It's already happening," Andrea answered.

"What do you mean?" Jan said.

"YouTube, for one. Then we have Facebook, Pinterest, Flickr, and many more Internet sites. People are making their histories and knowledge available to the world as permanent videographic records of their lives and interests. It's like every page on Facebook is in your head, projected to the world."

Andrea wasted no time insisting that more learning should be videographic. She favored lectures taught online by people such as Salman Kahn with his virtual Kahn Academy and websites like Skillshare where you can learn from others how to make, build, and create things.

She added, "Kahn stepped outside the education box, and is profoundly altering traditional teaching methods. In your words, Dennis, they are executing the less impossible."

"Can you explain that? Jan said.

"With so much recorded knowledge, we need to rethink the idea of a teacher in front of the class delivering a lesson. Now students can watch a Kahn lecture at home or at school and work later with the teacher in class to answer questions related to the lecture. More of these lectures, or learning modules, can be created by the best communicators in their fields."

I asked, "Who else is doing this sort of thing?"

"I like Brian Johnson's book, *A Philosopher's Notes*, and his website at entheos.com," she said. "Brian makes it easy to understand the great philosophers and thinkers of our time. His Entheos Academy for Optimal Living is a collection of freelance thinkers and gurus who teach courses in everything from nutrition to happiness. I also like Western Governors University, and the Great Courses series from what used to be the Teaching Company, and also MIT OpenCourseWare—all worth investigating. And there is iTunesU, which is loaded with great ideas to help teachers design and post their own courses on the web using audio and video files from over three hundred colleges and universities around the world. The resources are endless."

"The sources you just mentioned," I said, "sound like self-selected learning programs for adults, who either know what they want to do with their lives, or they are in full-search mode. What about elementary and high school kids? Many of them don't have a clue about what they want to do. They want to play sports, spend time on video games, listen to music, and hang out with their friends. Like we did. We know about the Kahn Academy, but what about programs that can turn kids on to learning?"

"The key to teaching adolescents is understanding what they *want* to learn and delivering it in the form they want to consume it. When children are interested in music, they will learn the names, recordings, and life histories of every artist in a genre. The schools need to build on that sort of passion and use it to springboard learning, not shut it down because it doesn't fit the curriculum."

Jan said, "Andrea, what would you do to change how subjects are taught?"

"First, I would hire the best producers, actors, and writers to make videos on every basic subject and make them available worldwide to all schools. Kahn Academy does a great job of using the Internet, so why not get our best communicators, artists, and musicians involved in teaching every subject on the Internet? Forget textbooks. Create a lot more interactive projects to engage kids, even *gamify* the lessons."

"What is gamify?" Ed asked.

"It's using games to teach complex relationships. *Sim City*, for example, is one of the oldest. It helps us learn about interdependence by simulating the real world. Young people love games because they challenges them to think. Universities and businesses use games to teach. Private schools use them. Why not public schools? Pick a subject, any subject, and use storytelling and games to deliver learning disguised as entertainment."

"Education by Hollywood?" said Jan.

"Yes. Teachers could be the moderators, curators, and tutors with more time to guide children to master their interests.

Once we ignite an interest—any interest—curiosity will take its natural course. All knowledge is connected."

Ed, the other man in our little group, said, "My wife taught fifth grade thirty years ago. She knew that the basal readers, the standardized books used for everyone in the class, didn't hold the interest of half the students. She wrote a grant for money to buy children's books in ten genres—mysteries, animals, whatever—and let them experience a book in each genre. It took a lot of extra time for her to build her library of hundreds of books, but the program was a huge success. Pre- and post-testing showed that all of the children at least doubled their reading ability, and some children were reading at three and four grades above their beginning levels. Is this what you're talking about?"

"Absolutely. If it's possible to design our own individual shoes online, why can't we individualize education?"

Jan, the apparent skeptic in the group, asked, "Are teachers prepared for individualized education?"

"Like everyone, teachers will need to adapt to learn new skills. Most of the young teachers coming out of school already have the skills. All teachers are different, and some are better than others. One of the most important factors in learning is having an effective teacher. We need the best teachers and speakers in the world delivering our learning materials. We have a new form of interactive textbook being promoted by Apple using their iBooks *Author* software that incorporates every medium, and it links to the Internet."

"This sounds like *Sesame Street* for all ages," I said.

"That's a good analogy. One of *Sesame Street's* secret

strengths is repetition. In our current education system, if the student doesn't grasp a concept in the first lesson or lecture—too bad. The teacher doesn't have time to give the lecture twice. Teachers have extensive material to cover. They have to move on. In the teachers' defense, it's also not easy to deliver the same material year after year, knowing that some children are falling behind. But imagine if you could put the lecture in the hands of the students, so they can pause and rewind the information until they've mastered a concept. As an added bonus, if a student is dyslexic, he will learn better by watching or listening to a demonstration.

"It doesn't matter whether you are a child or an adult, learning is about connecting to the presentation. Teacher quality can make all the difference in holding the students' attention. But teachers aren't trained speakers or great actors. We all know the difference between a boring speaker and one that inspires. Social media is turning us all into visual and auditory learners. We need great storytellers to deliver ideas and keep students engaged."

Jan asked, "How would schools afford all of this talent?"

"The cost of one lecture by a great presenter could be spread over thousands of schools as it is with textbooks. Also, friends of mine in the media tell me that a lot of educational material is already produced and archived. The History and National Geographic channels have hoards of educational material in their vaults. Students would share ideas in online forums and teach each other with a qualified teacher as a true facilitator rather than a babysitter or cop."

Ed said, "Will we even have schools as we know them?

Will teachers become consultants and form professional groups like investors or doctors with offices and meeting rooms in commercial buildings or malls?"

Andrea replied, "Sure. We need to think differently. Use our imaginations to find the money to provide every child with a tablet computer, and create learning environments that don't group students by age. Adult education classes thrive with students of all ages. Why is that so hard to imagine? In a rural one-room schoolhouse, the teacher still prepares lessons for multiple grade levels and advances the lessons at each student's pace. We must stop educating children the way we mass produce widgets in a factory."

I asked, "What about the content, Andrea? Will that change, too?"

"Schools still need to teach basic math and language skills, but I would also teach more creative problem solving and critical thinking skills to prepare children to handle the future, the unexpected, the unknown. If students learn how to apply and combine convergent and divergent thinking, they can use their skills to solve real-world issues. At the present time, children learn too many useless facts, often simply because facts can be tested. We must stop teaching to the tests and stop testing the irrelevant."

She was holding an empty glass in one hand. I was going to offer to refill it for her when a man approached and whispered something to her. She nodded and said to him, "Just a minute. I want to finish here, then I would be happy to meet with them." I wondered if she was someone important. In this town you never know who will turn up at a party.

After a few deep breaths she turned back to me and said, "Human beings are innately curious. We love to learn, but we do it best when we are acting as consumers, learning what interests *us,* not what an education system says we need. We all have our abilities and disabilities, but we stuff everyone into the same box and turn them into numbers, testing to see who is above or below average. What is the point? We can't let learning be about the politics of comparing test scores.

"We shouldn't be punishing children who struggle to read words on a page. People aren't stupid because their brains are wired to see patterns rather than words and letters, or because they are auditory learners."

Her friend was urging her to go with him, still anxious to introduce her to someone.

"How do you learn best?" I asked her.

She smiled and took off her dark glasses. I stared at her for a moment; then I felt stupid. I had no idea, not even a clue during our conversation, that she was blind. "I'm sorry," I said trying to think of something to say.

She laughed. "Don't apologize. I hope your book is a big success. I'll be listening for it." With that, she took her companion's arm and walked away.

Mary Lou appeared beside me and slipped her hand into mine. "She seemed very passionate. Was she interesting?"

"Very."

"What did she have to say?"

"She said we need to open our eyes."

Meaning of Survival

"You don't just wheel up to the SS office and put your hand out. The money comes from somewhere out there in the electrosphere."

While I was standing in line at a Jack in the Box and waiting for a #1 Combo (no onions, no special sauce), I noticed this fellow in a wheelchair roll by the door and park in the shade of a Palo Verde tree.

Looking up at the menu above the counter I read that the damage for my favorite meal runs about a thousand calories. I was not concerned, however, because I only eat this way every few weeks. I drink the regular Coke rationalizing that occasionally my low blood sugar needs a boost.

The combo is cheaper than ordering the sandwich, fries and drink separately. I don't eat all the fries, but it's still less money to buy the combo. I don't grasp the economics, but who can?

They called my number. I picked up my burger and fries and found a seat. I was about to bite into the burger, when I looked out the window and saw the guy in the wheelchair slumped over. I couldn't tell if he was sleeping or passed out. His hair was long and stringy. His mustache, scraggly beard and dirty camouflage jacket made him look like he had spent forty days and forty nights in the desert.

A large garbage bag hung off the back of his chair. Crushed soda cans looked ready to spill out. Watching him made me feel guilty. Looking at my burger, then back at the wheelchair guy, then back at my burger, my feelings of guilt shifted into overdrive. Finally, disgusted with myself, I went back to the order counter and asked them for a sack. I stuffed the fries, burger and napkins into the sack, then I walked outside to hand it over to my wheelchair guy.

He was still slumped in his chair, so I stood over him for a few seconds waiting for him to look up. I didn't want to wake him, so I laid the sack on his lap and placed the drink on the pavement next to his chair. I started to walk away when I heard him say, "Thank you." I looked back, and he was staring up at me. I asked him if he was okay.

"Just resting my eyes," he said. "Like to join me?" He motioned toward the grass next to his wheelchair.

I felt a little uneasy as I took a seat, actually worried the automatic sprinklers might come on.

He opened the sack and looked inside, then he lifted it up to his nose and took in a deep breath, as if the sack was an oxygen mask and he was on life support. He lowered the sack and looked at me and said, "Never get tired of that beautiful aroma. Have you eaten?" Now he was worried about me. He didn't sound like I had imagined.

"I was going to eat the burger," I said. "But you looked like you needed it more."

"Feeling sorry for me?"

"As a matter of fact..."

"You can say it. I'm not offended. But I don't feel sorry for me. No reason you should." He gave me a wry smile. "After all, who has the burger and fries?"

He had me there. He picked out a couple of fries and held them out for me. I looked at his hands, caked with black grime. He saw my hesitation, reeled in the offering, and stuffed the fries into his mouth. Then he reached into the sack and pulled out the paper sleeve full of fries and held them out for me to take a few. "Sorry," he said. "I'm a little off my game right now. It's hard to keep my hands clean. I had gloves, but yesterday they gave up the ghost. Wore out right here in the palms." He put his palms down on the wheels, and I understood.

"What's your name?" I asked.

"Terry. Yours?"

"Dennis. Mind if I ask what happened to you, Terry?" I motioned toward the wheelchair.

"Sure, but first you tell me what happened to you!" He smiled when he saw my surprise. "Just pimpin' you," he said.

He made me smile. He offered me a bite of the burger, but I declined. "You know what?" I said, "I think I will get another one. I'll be right back. Hold my seat, okay?"

He was chewing, so he just nodded.

I returned with a sack and drink of my own. I changed my order to the Ultimate Breakfast Sandwich, another one of my favorites.

We sat together eating, sipping our drinks, nodding our approval for the tasty food. He was mostly skin and bones, so I knew he wasn't worried about cholesterol. When he finished eating, he wiped his mouth with a napkin, patted his stomach, and thanked me. I nodded as I ate.

I was curious about his camo jacket. I pointed at it and asked him if he had been in the service. He said that he had not. He got the jacket for two bucks at the nearby Goodwill Store.

I asked him again, "So what happened? Why are you in the chair?" This time he answered while I ate.

"Motorcycle," he said.

I guessed he was in an accident. "How long ago?"

"Six years this fall."

"Is this how you live, collecting cans?"

"Yeah, mostly. But I eat pretty good—sometimes." He smiled and held up the empty sack.

"You get any disability payments?"

"Nope."

"Why not?"

"Long story."

"I've got a few minutes."

"Okay," he said, but he sounded a little irritated by the question. I was curious about why he didn't get government help. It was there to assist people in his situation.

"Don't have a bank account," he said. "No address, either."

"Where do you live?"

"A bunch of us camp in a lemon orchard."

"The owner doesn't care?"

"Nope. He lets us live there. We pick up lemons that fall on the ground. Keeps fruit rats away. We trade the lemons for different stuff."

"So what about Social Security? I think you could be

getting some payments." I thought so because I once looked into it for someone who was disabled.

"If you don't have a bank account or an address, you can't get anything," he said. "You don't just wheel up to the SS office and put your hand out. The money comes from somewhere out there in the electrosphere." He waved his hand up toward the sky. "Besides, I'm doing fine."

Talk about a survivor. "You don't have anyone to receive your payments for you? No family?"

"Nope." He looked around nervously and rocked his chair back and forth like he was finished with the small talk and ready to go.

"You need to be somewhere?"

"No, I need to go, like in GO!"

I realized he meant the toilet. "Let me open the door for you," I said, thinking he'd use the men's room inside.

He shook his head. He reached behind the chair to a little wire basket and produced an empty, wide-mouth bottle. He pointed toward an opening between buildings in the strip center across from Jack's. "I'll go back there. And hey, man, thanks for the meal. It's worth quite a few cans. Good thing I don't need gas for this buggy." He handed me his empty sack and asked me to toss it in the trash for him. "Thanks again for the #1 Combo. It's my favorite."

"Hey, Terry! Listen. Let me help you with Social Security. Maybe I can…" Before I could finish, he started rolling away. With his back to me, he raised his hand and waved goodbye.

I see Terry from time to time, rolling his wheelchair down the highway or at a gas station, rummaging in the trash bins by the pumps. I buy him an energy drink or a soda now and then. He said he prefers soda in a can because he can get a few pennies for the empty.

I didn't ask Terry what he would do if he could play God. Could he step out of his lifebox and change? Metaphorically speaking, sure, but he didn't want to change his life. That's a choice, too. Still, I know what I would do if I were God. I'd tell Social Security to arrange with Jack to give Terry a #1 Combo any time he wanted.

Autograph Please

*"God?" he said. "How could I be God? That's weird.
What kinda question is that?"*

One Saturday evening I was standing in the lobby of the Philadelphia Marriott Hotel. Mary Lou and I were attending a conference, and she was at a table consulting with a client about an editing project. We hadn't decided where to eat dinner, but I was hoping she would finish soon because I was hungry.

I noticed a young black kid sitting by himself in the lobby. He looked about fifteen and wore a Phillies baseball shirt bearing the number 35.

The kid was rolling a baseball over in his hands, checking his grip on the ball, pretending to pitch it. He looked bored. I was curious, so I walked over with my folded newspaper in hand and sat down in a chair at a ninety-degree angle to him. He snuck a peek at me but didn't say anything. I could have picked any one of the other ten chairs in the area. I wondered if he was considering why I sat down so close to him.

When I looked over at him, he nodded at me.

"How's it going? I see you're a pitcher."

His cautious eyes opened wider. "How you know that?"

"I used to be a pitcher when I was your age. I can see the way you grip the ball: two fingers on the seams, then across the seams. Infielders and outfielders don't do that."

He nodded and studied his grip. "You any good?" he said.

"I was okay, for a small town kid. Not like big city boys."

Again he nodded agreement. "Where you play?"

"In Wyoming. A town called Sheridan."

"Yeah, I know Wyoming. Guy from my neighborhood went to Wyoming. Point guard. He was *gooood*! I wanna go to St. Joe's. My dad's in the Marines, so I need to stay home right now . . . take care of my mama."

We didn't speak for a few minutes. Then he said, "I'm waitin' on Cole Hamels. My mama said he here today. I want him to sign my ball. His name worth a lot right now."

"You collect autographs?"

He shook his head, "Naw. First one. Might be worth somethin'—he stay hot."

"Could be. How long have you been waiting?"

"Time you got?"

"Little after six."

"My mama work here. We came 'bout lunch. She off at eight. She clean the rooms. You should see our house. It's *sooo cleeean*. I gotta make my bed every day—like she do it here."

I was surprised at how engaging he was—even more surprised that he had heard of Wyoming. I decided to ask him my favorite question, but I had a feeling it would come out a little less weird if I made it sound like a game.

"You want to play a game?"

He shrugged.

"It's a question and answer game. It might sound like I'm coming out of left field on this, but you seem like a bright guy, so I'd be interested in your answer."

He sat up and looked at me. "Baseball question?"

"No, it's a God question."

He wrinkled up his face like he hadn't heard me right. "Say what?" He sat forward in his chair.

I said, "If you could be God, right now, what would you do?"

"God?" he said. "How could I be God? That's weird. What kinda question is that?"

"But what if you could?"

"Can't happen. God is God. Can't nobody else be God."

"Okay, let me ask the question in a different way. What if God gave you a chance to do anything you wanted? What would it be?"

"You mean like the genie? I get three wishes?"

"That works for me. What three things would you do?"

Without hesitation he said, "Well, first, I wish God would buy this hotel for my mama, so she don't have to work so hard."

I wanted to tell him that was a good choice. "Okay, what else?"

He thought for a minute. "I already wished God bring my dad home safe. He's in Somalia. That's in Africa."

I nodded.

"I'm gonna ask God for that again. You think that's okay?"

"I think that's fine."

"Hope so."

I waited a moment because I could tell he was giving extra consideration to his final wish. "You have one more wish."

"I know." He slumped back in the chair and looked at the ceiling for a few beats. Then he sat up and tossed the ball in the air and caught it a couple of times. He was definitely thinking this one over.

"What's it going to be?" I said.

He looked at me, then at the ball. He held it out to me and he said, "What you think this be worth if God signed it?"

All I could say was, "Priceless!"

Unconditional

"When you came into the store and asked me what I would do if I could be God, I thought about how much I'd give to redo the last two years."

One afternoon Mary Lou asked me to go shopping with her. We went to an anniversary event at a small boutique she likes in The Gardens on El Paseo in Palm Desert. When we walked in, the salespeople greeted her by name. I had a pretty good idea why. Five minutes later it was like a party. Mary Lou was soon trying on clothes, drinking champagne, and chatting with other customers. Women know how to shop.

I started talking to one of the saleswomen that I will call Jessie. She seemed a little down and wasn't taking part in the fun. After a few minutes, she asked me if I liked shopping with my wife. I told her I actually did. She wanted to know what I might be doing that day if I weren't shopping. I figured she was trying to keep me entertained. I told Jessie I would be working on a book I was writing. She asked what it was about. I told her the idea and asked her what she would do if she could be God.

She stiffened and her eyes fluttered, not like she was flirting, or had picked up some dust, but like she was startled. I wondered if it was something I said.

"Did I say something wrong?" I asked.

"Wrong? No." She shook her head, touched her nose with the back of her hand, and looked about to cry. "I'm sorry," she said and hurried away.

That felt weird. One of the other salespeople came over to me and asked what happened. I just shrugged. She chased after Jessie while I waited and wondered what was going on. Then I picked up a magazine and thumbed through it.

After I watched a few rounds of Mary Lou modeling clothes, Jessie reappeared. It was obvious that she had been crying. She told me she had thought about my question and wanted to know what other people said when I asked them. Now I was reluctant to say anything. I was anxious about upsetting her again.

"Well . . . I get a lot of the same answers and a lot of different ones. Most people want to stop wars, heal the planet, and feed the hungry."

"Has anyone ever said they wanted to save a single person?"

"No, I haven't heard that, yet."

"Do you think that's being selfish?"

"To want to save someone's life? Not at all."

"Even though it wouldn't change the world or prevent war?"

"You know what . . . I think you should do what makes you feel best."

She nodded a couple of times. Then she looked like she was going to cry again. I didn't know what to say. Once again she rushed off into a back room, leaving me with the mystery.

Twenty minutes later Mary Lou was finished, and we paid the bill. I won't tell you how much it was, but I was thinking about invoking my God privilege. One of the saleswomen walked out with us, stopping a few yards outside the store entrance.

She said to me, "I want to thank you. I don't know what you said to Jessie, but she has been so depressed since her sister died. This is her first day back. She wouldn't talk to any of us about it. She told me you said something to her that helped. Then she called her brother-in-law. She's still on the phone."

"Is she okay?"

"She seems a lot better. At first I heard a lot of crying, but that stopped. Now she is just talking."

"What did you say to Jessie?" Mary Lou asked me.

"I asked her what she would do if she could be God."

The woman frowned. "Why did you ask her that?"

"I'm writing a book based on the answers I get to the question, so I ask everyone I meet. Please tell her I'm sorry if I upset her, but I'm glad she is feeling better."

The lady paused and stared at me. The she said, "That is an interesting question—about being God. I need to think about that." Then she added, "Well, thanks for coming in. I will tell Jessie that you asked about her." She hugged us both and we left.

As we walked away, Mary Lou said to me, "I dropped into the store a few days ago, and someone asked me if I knew that Jessie's sister had died. I didn't think to mention it to you. Sorry if you felt blindsided."

"No, don't worry about it," I said.

"It sounds like you helped her. Maybe there's a reason you were supposed to come with me today."

***

Two days later I stopped at a local coffee shop and was surprised to see Jessie sitting at a table by herself. She was stuffing a card into an envelope and looked up at me as she licked the envelope. She looked surprised; then she motioned for me to join her.

I approached her, feeling a little apprehensive. I don't like to make women cry.

She rose from her chair and gave me a warm hug like we were old friends. "I can't believe you just walked in here. This is amazing!"

"Really," I said. "Do you live around here?"

"No, but I love the stationery store in the back of this shopping center. I can't believe that you appeared right at this moment."

"Why is that?"

"Because I just finished writing this note to you. I wanted to thank you for helping me the other day. I can't believe what a coincidence it is to see you here. When you walked in, I wasn't sure it was you. But here you are." She handed me the envelope. "Don't open this until you get home."

"Well, thank you, though I have no idea what I did to deserve a card." I felt awkward.

"Do you have a moment?" she asked. She motioned for me to sit down. I pulled up a chair and joined her.

"I wanted to talk to you more the other day, but I was on the phone with my brother-in-law when you left. I was going to thank you for what you said. When you asked me what I would do if I were God, I thought about my sister."

"I'm sorry. I heard about it as we were leaving the store."

Jessie picked up a napkin and used it to wick away a tear that was forming in one eye. "She was hit by a car when she was on her bike. They took her to the hospital, but she had really bad internal injuries. She was gone in less than two hours. I never had a chance to say goodbye."

"Oh, I am sorry."

"Angela was my only family. I was so depressed because I didn't have the money to fly out to the funeral. My brother-in-law couldn't afford to buy me a ticket, either. I have been so worried about her."

She paused as if she was expecting me to say something. I waited.

She continued, "For the past two years I have been trying to get her to go back to church. A year ago she said she didn't believe in God anymore. I quit talking to her so she would get the message to shape up and hold on to her faith. But instead of turning her around, it split us in two. It was so stupid on my part, and so wrong. When you came into the store and asked me what I would do if I could be God, I thought about how much I'd give to redo the last two years. So when I was in back, at the store, I decided to call my brother-in-law and tell him why I hadn't returned any of his calls."

She suddenly stopped talking. She looked at me with glassy eyes and touched my hand. She apologized for tearing up, then took a tissue from her purse. She wiped away her tears, careful not to smudge her mascara. Then she said, "When I told Justin, my brother-in-law, how afraid I was that Angela wouldn't be in heaven, he told me why he kept calling me. He wanted me to know that just before she passed, she asked for a priest to give her the last rites. Oh my God! I was so happy! So relieved! I can't tell you how happy I was . . . even though she was gone." She paused a moment and took a breath, then she continued. "You asked me what I would do if I could be God, and I never answered you," she said. "But now I know what I would do. I wrote it in the note I gave you."

I waited for her to continue.

She said, "If I could be God, I would tell the world—I would tell everyone—that nothing is more important than loving someone for who they are. It doesn't matter if they believe in God, or not. I would say never—ever—make someone's faith a condition for loving them."

BDO

"If I could be God," he started in again, "I would give everyone a BDO."

Mary Lou got up early one Saturday morning and decided to wash all of the windows in our house. They needed it, and I had been talking about doing it since a dust storm had spotted them a few weeks before. Window washing is normally my job, but she knew I hadn't been sleeping well lately, so she wanted to surprise me. I confess I felt like a sloth, not cleaning them myself. However, during our thirty-five years of marriage, I have found that it is better to let her know how much I appreciate her, than to feel guilty about shirking my duties. I promised myself to reciprocate, but that is another story.

On this particular day I decided to work on my book, so I called a friend to see if he could give me any ideas. His name is Alvaro, which means "noble guardian" in Spanish.

He picked up the phone after three rings. I usually get his voice mail. "Hey!" I said. "You picked up!"

"The magic of caller ID You even have your own ring tone. Did I tell you that?"

"Yes, and I'm flattered—the theme from *The Exorcist*.

Hey, I need to ask you a question. Do you have a moment?"

"It's Saturday. I have all the moments you need, my friend."

"Great. I am writing this book about what people would do about their lives, or the world, if they could be God."

"Really?" he said. I could hear him thinking. Not because he thinks louder than other people, but he had a tone in his voice that said, I am really wondering about you.

I said, "I am curious. What you would do?"

"If I could be God? Why do you want to know this?"

"Because you are a unique person, and I am looking for unique points of view."

"I see. Is this another one of the ways you fill your time while you are waiting to die?"

"Exactly," I said.

"What if I don't want to be God? This is a position of great authority and responsibility."

"It's just for today. I think you can handle it."

"Do I have to cure all the ills of the world?"

He is a high school teacher. I imagined him writing lesson plans at his computer or grading papers. "No," I said, "You can just make me a burrito the next time I come over."

"Hmmm. Hardly worthy of my godly abilities. What if I thought of something slightly more meaningful?"

"Whatever you want."

He was quiet for a moment, which is normal. I know this is a hard question to answer. Some people don't even want to answer. Some people want to solve every problem in existence; others get very specific and personal. Most don't know where to start. Maybe they think I am judging their choices. I try not to give that impression, but I realize the question implies gravitas.

"Okay," he said. "Right after I took care of war, starvation, cancer, and my ex-wife, I would banish all video games."

"Why video games?" I didn't care to ask about his ex-wife.

"Because they are poisoning families."

"How so?"

"People never talk to each other anymore. They rarely spend any time together. People are hiding in their own little cocoons. I would also require all texting to be done in complete sentences and limit it to ten minutes a day. I would require kids to play outside at least two hours per day. I would eliminate all snack foods and sodas. And I would make both the girls and the boys hike their pants back up to their waists so I don't have to look at their underwear. I forgot to ask, would these changes just last for one day, or would they be permanent?"

"It's up to you. Your world."

Alvaro has been teaching for more than twenty years. He complains a lot about distractions, about how hard it is to hold students' attention in class. I have heard these complaints many times. The fact that he would use his supreme powers this way did not surprise me. But I was looking for more from him.

I asked the magic question. "Is there anything else?"

"Yes," he said. He paused for a moment. "I would find my daughter. I know that's selfish, but . . ." His voice was spiked with sorrow and a hint of anger.

"Alvaro!" I said. "Imagining you have God's power doesn't mean you can't do something personal. It's a metaphor."

His daughter from his second marriage would be sixteen now. She ran away from home a year ago. He hasn't heard from her since. He and his wife divorced, partly over that. She said their girl, Tanya, left home because Alvaro was too strict. He said it was because his wife was too permissive. He had experienced a lot of heartache with family issues—I won't go into all of them here. It sounded to me like he was trying to get more control of his life.

"If I could be God, I would . . ." His words trailed off. I had a feeling he was going to say something that he thought I might not want to hear. I waited a moment, but he didn't say anything more. I regretted stirring up his pain.

"If I could be God," he started in again, "I would give everyone a BDO."

"You want to explain that?"

"Best Day Over. BDO. When things feel like they are just too much, you can invoke your right to have your Best Day Over. You can summon the joy you felt from the best day of your life. You can use this whenever you want, as many times as you need it."

"Nice." I said, trying to imagine what would be my best day. Then I asked him, "What is your BDO?"

"Hasn't happened yet."

"Really? You haven't had a best day in your life?"

"My best day will be the day Tanya returns home. I know she is out there somewhere. I pray she is okay. I am reserving my BDO for that day. When I see her, I want to be able to enjoy that day for the rest of my life."

The Producer

"Now if I could make Iron Man into a relationship picture—everybody in the business would think I was God."

In La Quinta, California where I live, you can meet a lot of creative people including producers, writers, actors and others in the film industry who own or rent second homes in the desert. One morning I called a producer friend to ask him what he would do if he could be God. In the movie business, producers need to act the part to get their pictures made, so I thought he might add some special seasoning to my question.

"Make it quick!" That was what he always he said when answering his cell phone.

"Hi, Jerry! It's Dennis Green."

"Hey, how's it hangin', buddy?

You have to get right to the point with Hollywood folks. "I know you're busy, but I'd like to ask you a question."

"*Okaaaay.* I hope it's not serious. You getting divorced?" He says that every time we talk. It's a running joke. Ironically, the chances of it being true are pretty good in his business. Fortunately, I am not in his business.

"Jerry, if you could be God, how would you change your life, or what would you do to make the world a better place?"

"I've already got two scripts in development, young guy from Encino. Helluva writer. Maybe you've got something, maybe not. We could do a treatment—see where it goes. What else you got?"

"I'm not pitching a script, Jerry. I'm writing a book. I am asking people what they would do if they could play God."

"Why?"

"To help you step out of your lifebox and unleash your imagination."

"The only box I care about is a box office."

"I've seen your pictures."

"Meaning?"

"You make relationship pictures."

"So?"

"So they aren't typically big box office. If all you cared about was the money, you'd make movies like *Iron Man*."

"Now if I could make *Iron Man* into a relationship picture—everybody in the business would think I *was* God." He laughed. "By the way, what do you do all day? You sit around thinking up nutty stuff like this? Why don't you bring me something I can sink my teeth into?" He delivered the last line with his very acceptable Kirk Douglas imitation. Jerry was obsessed with the great actor.

"I'll work on something for you," I said.

"My uncle had a piece of *Spartacus*." He said it like he had invested in the film himself. It was the Hollywood way. Anyone who actually made money investing in a picture was a rare bird indeed. It also meant they had "juice." In Tinseltown it's all about who you know or are related to.

"Lucky him," I said, knowing that Jerry was referring to the 1960 version of *Spartacus* starring Kirk Douglas—not the recent Starz television series.

"By the way, does this pay?" Jerry said.

"Does what pay?"

"This idea of yours."

"You mean pay you?"

"Time is money, my friend."

"Jerry. It's a simple question. I'm not asking you to rewrite *The Ten Commandments*."

"Now that was a picture!" Pause. "Okay, okay! Call Sally, and she'll write something up for you."

Sally was his personal assistant. "You're going to have Sally tell me what you would do if you were God?"

"To Sally, I am God. Look, I gotta go."

A few minutes later I sent Sally an e-mail summarizing my conversation with Jerry. I wasn't expecting much, but you never know.

I worked awhile then decided to make a sandwich while I watched CNBC to see how much money I was losing. Mary Lou had taken her mother to the doctor, so I was on my own. I slapped together a ham and cheese sandwich, sat down, and turned on the TV.

Coincidentally there was a story about how hard it is for independent producers to get films green-lighted by major studios. What a brutal business! I finished my lunch and went back to work on a different book.

Two hours later I checked my e-mail and saw a message from Sally. The subject line read—If Jerry Was God.

I opened the message.

Hi, Dennis,

Your idea about dreaming the impossible is interesting. When you asked me what I thought Jerry would do if he was God, it made me smile because Jerry already thinks he is God. And whatever impossible project he dreams up, he expects me to make it possible.

Why don't you call Jerry back and ask him what he would do if I was God.

Warmest regards,

Sally

Discovery

"It doesn't hurt me, so why should I mind? I love him. He's a great guy." She paused and smiled again. It was a wry smile. "But it is funny to watch."

Our niece, Brooklin, came to visit us one day. She and her husband, John, live about ninety miles away. He was out of town, but she brought their son, AJ, to show him off and stay with us for a few days. We hadn't seen them since AJ was born two months ago at a hospital near our house. He had arrived a few weeks early while she was visiting, and AJ's doctors had kept him at the hospital for an extra week to gain strength and weight. During that somewhat guarded period, Brooklin and John stayed with us. As a result, we feel especially close to all three.

Brooklin was filling us in on AJ's latest babyhood feats: smiling, turning over, and trying to stick his foot in his mouth—something I am familiar with from my years of meetings with people much smarter than me.

I asked her how it felt to create something so magical as a human being. She laughed and said the process was a bit harrowing, but she was lucky to have a fabulous coauthor to share the adventure.

She marveled at how everything was a first for AJ—first time he smiled, first time he grabbed her finger, first time he rolled over. She loved creating his day and being a part of his discoveries. She was a high school teacher on maternity leave and wouldn't go back to the classroom until the following semester. She said she was just beginning to think about her students again. During a lull in the conversation, I told her about my book, and I asked her what she would do if she could be God.

Being a thoughtful person, she said she would have to think about it. So we went on talking about other stuff. I asked her how John was doing with his new job. John was telecommuting, working from home for the first time, so she was able to watch his work routine while she was still home all day. She was amazed at his discipline—keeping phone appointments, making sales calls, talking to customers like he was in an office downtown.

"You know he does everything in fives," she said, as if it was common knowledge.

"No," I said. John is one of my favorite people, but this was news to me. "What do you mean, he does things 'in fives?'"

"Oh, you didn't know?" She was clearly surprised that we didn't know everything about John. She explained, "If he is emptying the dishwasher, he will remove five things at a time."

"You mean he will put five forks or five knives away, or five glasses and then five plates in some kind of order?"

"No, he puts away a total of five things, no matter what they are, then he cleans the counter, then he might go in the bathroom and clean that counter, then he might sit down and read one chapter in a book or one magazine article, then he might walk the dog. That completes a set of five things. After that he will come back to the dishwasher and put away five more items to begin another cycle of fives."

"When did you discover this about John?"

"I first noticed it after we started living together. One day he was clearing out the dishes, and he put a few things away—five to be exact. Then he went into the family room and started watching a football game on TV. I followed him into the room and asked him if he was going to finish unloading the dishes. He said he wouldn't do them right then because he had already done five. I told him I didn't get it, so he explained how he does everything in this pattern of five things at a time." She held up her hand with five fingers spread wide to emphasize the number.

"I never noticed," I said.

"Because you don't live with him."

"Does this bother you?" I asked.

"No," she said, smiling. "It was just a surprise. At first I wondered why he didn't finish things, but I realized he actually did. It might take all day because he does a little of each chore and then moves on to the next. He's very organized. He reads books according to a schedule of genres. One fiction, then one biography, one sports, one history and so on. He's very well-informed and well-rounded."

"Do you ever jump in and finish something because you want it completed?"

"Sometimes."

"You know that Mary Lou and I are writing books about marriage, right?"

She nodded. "How's it going?"

"It's going well. In one chapter we talk about how difficult it is for many husbands and wives to tolerate each other's quirks. I think we all crave some kind of order, and we try to impose it on our partners so we will feel more comfortable and in control. It sounds like you understand John's routine and have adapted pretty well."

"It doesn't hurt me, so why should I mind? I love him. He's a great guy." She paused and smiled again. It was a wry smile. "But it is funny to watch. Or it was, but now I don't really think too much about it. Sometimes I finish up something he started, and he comes back later and finds it's done; that's okay with him, too. He just finds something else to complete his fives."

Later that evening Brooklin was giving AJ a bath in our bathroom sink. She used a thick towel as a cushion, spreading it under him. He laid back at an angle; his round tummy made him look like a little Buddha in his own private spa. He splashed away with his arms and legs pumping and palms slapping at the water. We were laughing about how perfectly the sink fit his little four-month-old body.

Out of the blue, Brooklin asked me, "How many people have answered your question about being God?"

"Quite a few. Why?"

"I'm guessing that you have the big stuff covered then, right?"

"The big stuff? Yes, if you are talking about disease, famine, and wars. A lot of people have said they would take care of those things. What are you thinking?"

"If all of the big stuff is covered, I'm thinking . . . if I could be God, I would make it possible for every baby and every husband on earth to be loved as much as I love mine."

Brooklin watched her son as she talked, never looking at me. He splashed away in his little sink tub, and my gaze was fixed on her face glowing with absolute, total, complete, and perfect joy. I thought about her decree and imagined all of the mothers' glowing faces, and all the happy babies and lucky husbands around the world who would be receiving heavy doses of love. Maybe that's all we need to make this life worth living.

Don't You Think?

"God gave us free will," she said. "We are the ones who can screw up this world, or make it better. Don't you think?"

Marylin works in a hair styling studio in Palm Desert, California. Because of her positive nature, I call her my "thairapist." No matter what I tell her, she nods and smiles, even laughs at my bad jokes.

According to Mary Lou, Marylin does a great job of styling my so-called "look." When I close my eyes, I visualize my look as a flowing mane. When I open them, I see a receding glacier. Climate change. I am thankful that Marylin does her best with what I've got.

I was sitting in her chair, and she was clipping away like a supermodel surgeon when I asked her what she would do if she could play God. She is used to me asking strange questions, but I was surprised when she became silent. I waited for her answer.

"I, uh, I don't feel comfortable with that question."

"Why?"

"Well, I just don't think that we should ever imagine we can be God."

I was curious. "Does it feel blasphemous?"

"Yes, I think so." She didn't elaborate. I could feel that she was struggling with this idea.

"It just doesn't feel right, she said. "I was raised to be respectful."

"I understand. Let me ask this. Have you ever created something?"

"Yes. I'd like to think so. That's my job. It's what I do."

"And wouldn't you call God the number one creator?"

"Yes," she said. Her voice was cautious, like she was driving happily down the road and suddenly was caught in a cloudburst.

"So whenever you create something, you are doing the same thing that God does, right? You're playing God."

"I guess so." She didn't sound convinced.

"Try the question this way. How would you feel about emulating God, doing things that God would approve of, working to create a good life for yourself and for others? Does that feel blasphemous?"

"I have no problem with that. I am sure that God wants us to be creative and do good things. Playing God just sounds strange, like we're cloning animals or something."

"What about actors who play God in a movie. Is that okay?"

"I think that's okay."

"So if you could emulate God's nature, would that be okay? Would you feel right about creating a better world or a better life for yourself or your family?"

"Well, sure," she said and was quiet for a moment before she spoke again. "Now I understand what you're saying. How would I improve things to make a better world? In that case, first I would cure all diseases. Next I would stop all the wars, then make sure that all of the hungry were fed." She stopped talking and looked at me in the full-length mirror on the wall in front of my chair. I think she was waiting to see my reaction. Had she done enough? Not done enough with my hair, but done enough as God. So I asked my extra question, "Is there anything else?"

"That's a lot already, don't you think?" Marylin likes to say, "Don't you think?"

Often I don't think, so it is an appropriate question. "It is, but you aren't limited to the big things. You could do anything. What about giving everyone in the world a good haircut?"

She scrunched her face and gave me a look that said cutting hair was beneath her status—not as Marylin, but as God. I decided to push her. "If you cured all of the diseases in the world, what disease would you start with?"

"I would do all of them at once."

"What do you think would happen if you ended all disease, all wars, and all starvation? Everything at once?"

"I would be very happy."

"I understand, but how would the world be different if all of those things were taken care of?"

"It would be great—don't you think?"

This question seemed to be weighing on her; maybe she was worrying that I didn't agree with her.

"Makes you wonder," I said.

"About what?"

"About why *God* doesn't do all of those things at once."

"God gave us free will," she said. "We are the ones who

can screw up this world, or make it better. Don't you think?"

"But you said, if you could be God, you would fix all of those problems. Why do you think God hasn't done it?"

She was cutting around my ear, so instead of answering my question, she told me a story about one of her clients who had a chunk missing from the top of his ear.

"He just sneezed," she said, throwing her head back and forward to imitate a sneeze. "It happened at a different studio where I used to work. His stylist was clipping around his ear, and—*sniiiiiip*—cut the top right off. There was blood everywhere. I had no idea we had so much blood in our ears, did you?"

I imagined blood and hair pooled on the tile floor. "Is that a hint for me to stop asking questions?"

"No!" she said with a little laugh. "I'm just warning you not to sneeze when I am snipping around your ears."

I shut up while she was trimming. I had no idea haircuts could be so dangerous. When she moved to the top of my head I asked, "Are we finished talking about God?"

"I'm thinking."

"While you are thinking, here's another question. Do you think God has a plan?"

"If you mean a plan for everything, I think so."

"Do you think God planned for us to fight wars, or get sick, or starve?"

"I think God planned for us to love each other, to share what we have, take care of our planet, and to eat right so we don't get sick."

"Why do you think the plan got so messed up?"

"Any plan can get messed up when you are dealing with

people. Don't you think?"

"I can't argue that point. If you were God, what would you do to encourage us all to do those things: share, take care of the planet, and eat right?"

"I would send a message that free will isn't going to be free anymore if you don't start making better choices."

"Will you take away my free will if I don't shape up?"

"No. I won't take it away. You will lose it automatically by how you live. I would just warn you that every freedom has a cost. If you don't learn to share, you won't have any friends. If you don't take care of the planet, it's going to die and your kids will suffer. If you don't eat right, you'll get sick, spend your life savings on health care, or die sooner than you should."

"I never thought free will could be so dangerous."

"It might be time for all of us to think again. Don't you think?"

All You Need to Know

"God is a concept, and that concept is very personal and different for everyone. It explains why we have thousands of different religions in the world."

Alison said, "What if we returned to the Garden of Eden and started over?" Alison was a friend visiting us from Dallas. We were talking about writing, and the conversation drifted to my book. Of course I asked her what she would do if she could play God.

She said, "When I was in college, I wrote an essay on the Book of Genesis. Back then I was already imagining what I would do if I were God. I rewrote the story and took Satan completely out of the picture. Why did God create Satan in the first place? I've read that Moses is the author of Genesis, so why do you think he created the Devil?"

"I have read that about Moses, too, but other scholars say a lot of people had a hand in writing Genesis—and that it took centuries to mold the story into what we read now."

"But do you think we need the Devil?" Alison said. "That was one of the big ideas in my essay. In my Eden, an apple was just another fruit, not an obedience test. I also never understood why

God was always testing people's loyalty in the Old Testament."

"I can't answer that one. But if you excluded the Devil in your essay, what did you do about Original Sin?"

"We don't need it when we're born in a state of grace."

I asked, "What about the Seven Deadly Sins?"

"Gone."

"We wouldn't feel greed, or envy, or gluttony, or any carnal desires?"

"No. If we started over without the snake, we could remain in Eden, enjoying life without fear of death. We would have everything we ever needed. Isn't that a better version of Genesis?"

"I don't know. Every good story needs a villain," I said. "Without the Devil your story is missing an antagonist. The creation story wouldn't be very compelling without a villain. I am having a hard time imagining the story of creation without a bad guy."

"I didn't."

"What grade did you get?"

"I got a C+."

I laughed. "Maybe your story didn't work without a villain."

Alison laughed with me.

We both went on laughing until she said, "My professor said it was a ridiculous premise, but he appreciated the fact that there were no typos."

We laughed some more.

Alison added, "I was an econ major at the time, and I was enamored of Adam Smith, the social philosopher."

"I read the *Wealth of Nations* a long time ago," I said.

"He also wrote the *Theory of Moral Sentiments* years before *Nations*. I used one of his moral sentiments in my essay's closing." She looked at the ceiling searching her memory, then she said, "His desire was to instill in every man, woman, and child the moral ability to love the good fortune of others, even though they would get nothing from it except the pleasure of seeing it."

"I like that. Was it for your econ class?"

"No, comparative religions. I thought it fit. Apparently I was wrong."

"If you had it to do over, would you write the same essay, add a few more footnotes, see if you could get a B+?"

"Not a chance." She laughed again.

"Okay, seriously, what would you do now if you were God?"

"I used to think that God should join all religions together and eliminate the hatred that leads to persecution and war. No more nasty periods in history such as the Crusades or the Spanish Inquisition. We could also put an end to conflicts between Christians and Muslims, between Muslims and Jews, and between Catholics and Protestants. Together, I thought we could direct massive coordinated efforts toward ending starvation and eradicating disease on a worldwide scale."

"You said you used to think you would get all the religions together. Does that mean you wouldn't do it today?"

"Now I think now that one world religion would be as bad as one world government."

"Because . . . ?"

"I realized, at some point, that the reason we have so many

religions is because God is not out there." She waved one arm in a big semicircle. "God is in here." She placed her hand over her heart. "And here." She pointed to her head. "God is not a being with shape or volume. God is a concept, and that concept is very personal and different for everyone. It explains why we have thousands of different religions in the world. We can't see God. We can only feel God's essence. I don't know how God feels to you, or how you perceive God, but I don't refer to God as 'him' because my God can't be represented by a pronoun. My God doesn't have a gender. When we imagine God in human form, we open the door to wondering where his mother is."

"You mean Mary?"

"No, not Jesus Christ's mother. I'm talking about God the Father. Where is his mother? If we give God the Father a physical form, don't we have to explain his origin?"

"Interesting perspective."

"Not everyone would understand my version of God. The Romans and Greeks had god smorgasbords, one for every fear or desire. Christianity popularized God in the human form of a young man with a beard and flowing robes. But it's hard for a lot of people to relate to this particular image."

"How would your God look?"

"My God is the sum total of all the ideals we call virtues. That's all I need to believe about God. I don't need God to be a Jew, or a Gentile, or to have a body."

"Do you think a formless God helps or hurts most people's chances of relating to God?"

"Giving God a form isn't necessary for me. The Holy Spirit has no fixed form."

"Which is why people seldom mention him. It's hard to wrap your mind around a spirit."

She grinned. "Or angels without wings. I get your point. I believe that we created Jesus Christ so we could have a concrete image of God. In the Bible it says that God told Moses not to look at his face, or he would die. I don't need a concrete image. I believe God is the organizing force in the universe, the glue that holds everything together. God is present in every star and every molecule and atom. God is the energy in every plant and animal including ourselves. When people say we are made in God's image—to me that means atoms, molecules, and genes—not flesh and bone."

"You sound like a Navajo."

Alison nodded and sat up on the edge of the sofa. "I have a t-shirt with a message screened on the front: 'I would rather spend my time in the mountains contemplating God, than be in church contemplating the mountains.'"

She paused and adjusted herself on the couch. I sensed she had more to say so I waited. Moments later she began again, "When I feel something deeply, or see someone doing something that makes me feel good—such as showing true courage or integrity, standing up to injustice, caring for someone who's ill, or building aqueducts over mountains to bring clean water to people living in jungles—I feel like God is a part of the transaction. In other words God is pure goodness that fills me. Do you know what I mean?"

"I think so."

"One definition of the word 'God' comes from the old English word 'good.' When I do something good, I feel God in me. A neurologist might say that my feeling is chemically induced by neurotransmitters and hormones, and that is fine. That's how we feel rewarded for doing good. For someone who wants to go somewhere to worship, pray, and share the religious experience, to feel close and be part of a like-minded community—I think that is great. But I don't require a church to feel God. I feel God's presence in my own individual way, in the good things I do. I know that sounds like a greeting card, but it is how I relate to God."

"Actually, Abraham Lincoln also said that 'good' was his religion. I think people would be interested in how you can feel a personal relationship with God, yet not practice any religion."

"As I said, my God is not a 'he,' or a king that demands tribute or worship. God represents goodness. When I do good for someone, I feel God. When I witness an act of kindness, I feel God. When I am loving, I feel God. When I am being fair, or generous, or virtuous in some way, I feel God. When I do something I'm not proud of, I feel God is missing. But I want to feel the God in me, so I do something that feels right and good."

"You make God sound like a drug."

"When I do something positive, it can feel like a drug. When I do something great, it can even border on euphoria. I say that goodness is a gateway drug to God. Psychologists would probably tell me this is my conscience, and that's okay, too. I equate conscience with God and with the soul. God is present in universal human virtues. Doing good is how I express the God in me."

"It sounds like my kind of religion. Clearly, you separate God from religion."

"Yes. I relate spirituality to moral values. That makes it a belief system, which is the core of any religion or culture. But I don't have any rituals, or dogma, or prayer books, or icons. No tithing. My God doesn't care about what I eat, or whether I should pay homage once a week, or ever. My God doesn't possess human faults, like being insecure about being praised or honored, or even denied. My God is a reflection of all the virtues that we find important and necessary for a functioning society."

"How do you distinguish good from bad—without a Bible, for example?"

"I live in a Judeo-Christian culture, so my morals begin there. We need shared moral values to get along with each other. The human race wouldn't survive unless we cooperated. On one side you have people who believe that morality comes from God. On the other side, you have people who believe morality is an evolutionary imperative, that we developed rules and laws to be able to survive together."

"What about a culture that advocates murder or suicide bombing? The Nazis had some screwed-up ideas about right and wrong. How does someone from that culture feel God?"

"I have no idea how anyone can feel good about mass murder. And I can't explain the actions of zealots, or criminals, or sociopaths, either. They are perversions. My idea of good wouldn't condone murder, suicide, or any of the Seven Deadly Sins."

"Does your God love you?"

Alison said, "My God is not watching me and approving or disapproving. God is in me, a part of me. If I could do anything to change the world, I would tell you to do what is right, what is kind, what is honest and caring, and you will never have to worry about what you think of yourself, or worry about looking over your shoulder. I say, don't be good because someone is watching you. Do good because it makes you feel God. That's all you need to know."

Who Cares?

"During the entire time with her, I felt like a tea kettle with the top glued on, ready to blow. I resented feeling that I was being taken for granted."

Leslie and Jack recently started a small group home for people who can no longer live alone. Because our nation's aging population is presenting families and societies with enormous challenges, they decided to tackle the problem in their own way by starting a home caregiving business. They bought a new house and made all of the improvements and changes required by local laws to accommodate five clients who need a place to live that provides 24/7 care. They call it Caring House.

I was talking to Leslie one day, asking how their new venture was coming along. I knew Jack and she were already caring for one ninety-year-old woman and another who was ninety-seven.

"You would not believe what I went through yesterday," she said, shaking her head. "Remember when you asked me a while ago about what I would do if I could be God, and I said I would think about it?"

"This doesn't sound good," I said, seeing her frown.

"Let me tell you what happened yesterday. Do you have a few minutes?"

"Sure."

"Well, this is how my day began. One of our placement services offered us a client before I had a chance to vet her, you know, to make sure she was a good fit for our other clients and us. I was told that this new client was a sixty-eight-year-old woman with slight dementia, and she couldn't live alone anymore. Since her brother lives out of state, he made the arrangements by phone with Anna, an agent there that I really trust. A week ago Anna met with her, and she said the woman seemed like a good fit for us, so I went along with her judgment.

"The client's brother called me yesterday and said his sister was being discharged from the hospital—that day. I told him I didn't know she was even in the hospital. She must have been admitted after Anna met with her because Anna didn't mention about the hospital. The brother asked if I could pick up his sister from the hospital and bring her to Caring House. He would make all of the arrangements with the hospital and phone his sister about me."

"But you hadn't met the woman?"

"No. I relied on Anna. Her job is to check out the clients and then bring them by our place for an interview. We all decide if it will work for everyone. We go over the costs, too, because the price is different for a private room versus a double room. But I wasn't able to meet with Anna or the client, and the brother couldn't come because he was working. I told the brother I would take her based on the agency's recommendation."

"But it sounds like you had some problems."

"The hospital was unbelievable. I went to get her, and they had already discharged her, but she didn't have any clothes." Leslie raised up her arms and shook her fists in the air in protest. "All she had to wear under her hospital gown was a pair of Depends, you know, the paper underpants."

"Your client with dementia and no clothes is leaving the hospital wearing only Depends and one of those gowns that opens in the back? What did the hospital say about her clothes? She must have been wearing something when they admitted her."

"Who knows?" Leslie said, rolling her eyes again. "They said they didn't know what happened to her clothes. According to one of the nurses, she was drunk when they admitted her. I don't know how she got there. The nurse said the woman had been in detox for the past three days, which I also knew nothing about. Maybe they tossed her clothes. All she had was this giant purse, so add that to your image. When I walked into her room, she was sitting there in a wheelchair, waiting for me to take her."

"What did you do?"

"First, she didn't have any paperwork. She is supposed to have certification for immunizations to live in a group home. When I learned she didn't have the papers, I phoned the agency but couldn't reach Anna. I called the brother, got voice mail. The discharge nurse was barking at me that he needed the room. So what do you think I did?"

"You took her."

"I had to. What was she going to do? She was skin and bones. Her hair looked like a Halloween wig. I couldn't leave the poor woman there."

"The hospital wouldn't keep her until you could figure something out?"

"No! They had already discharged her. I had no choice. So an aide wheeled her down to the front boarding area while I got my car. Picture me holding her hospital gown together in back while guiding her into the passenger seat, as she announces she wants to go home and get something to wear. I didn't know where she lived. Fortunately, her discharge papers showed an address. So I drove her there; it was an hour in the other direction from Caring House.

"When we finally pulled up in front of her house, she asked me for the key. I told her that I didn't have any keys to her home. She seemed a little paranoid, too. She wouldn't let me search her purse for a key. She thought she'd hidden a key somewhere outside but couldn't remember where. I searched the usual places: on the ledge over the door, under the doormat, under some large rocks in the flower bed. She even had one of those fake stones where you can hide a key—but it was empty."

"What did you do? Did she ever get any clothes?"

"Well, I tried the neighbors. But no one was home."

I waited a few beats, then shook my head, wondering where she was going with this story.

She continued telling the story. "I called her brother but got his voice mail again. I was flustered because I had another appointment—in an hour and a half—so I told her I would take her to our group home, and I would keep trying to reach her brother. Well, she would have none of that. She wasn't about to go anywhere in a hospital gown. Plus she needed new Depends. Hers were all wet . . . and I don't want to tell you how glad I am to have faux leather seats in my car."

About this time I was suppressing a laugh. I was already smiling, but none of this was funny to Leslie.

"She demanded that I take her to Target and buy her a muumuu—you know, one of those loose-fitting housecoats—plus new Depends. But she had no money. Okay, I can handle that. I left her in the car and went into Target. It took me twenty minutes, and I half-expected to come out of Target and find her gone, but she was still there, sitting in the passenger seat smoking a cigarette—in my car, which I just had detailed. I never let anyone smoke in my car, so I was going nuts about that. I asked her where she got the cigarette, and she said it was from the guy in the pickup who was parked next to me. I can't even imagine what that conversation was like."

Now I am picturing this as a movie and trying to imagine who would play the characters. I said, "So did you finally get her back to Caring House?"

"I did, thank God, but that wasn't the end of it. When we got to Caring House, she was supposed to pay the first month's deposit. She had her checkbook in her purse, and I told her the amount to write on the check."

"That's progress."

Leslie shook her head and raised one hand to her forehead. She looked up at me with a sardonic grin. "She wrote the check to herself."

I moaned in sympathy. "Amazing! So she had to write you another check?"

"No, she couldn't. She had no more checks. It was her last one in the book."

Now I was feeling frustrated.

"No, I am serious. But by this time, I am ready to just give up and do whatever . . . I tell her not to worry about it. I will talk to her brother, and we will work it out."

I interjected, "So all is well that ends well?"

"No!"

"Not the end?"

"Not by a long shot."

I shook my head.

"She says she will not be able to sleep until she pays what she owes. Her word is everything to her. She says she needs to go to the bank, and she walks out the front door, and I'm chasing after her trying to stop her, but she will have none of it. She gets in the car and sits there in her new muumuu. Then she gets back out of the car and hollers at me to bring her a cigarette. This very moment I see the daughter of another potential client, plus Anna from the agency, pull up in front of the house. It's the appointment I set up a week ago."

"What did you do?" I said.

"You wouldn't believe the rest of it, and it would take me another ten minutes to tell the story. I just wanted to tell you . . . if I could be God, I know exactly what I would do."

"What?"

"Have you ever heard the saying, 'I know God will never give me more than I can handle, but sometimes I wish he didn't have so much confidence in me?'"

"Yes."

"Well, after yesterday, I'm not sure God has any confidence left in me. I didn't handle things very well. As I am telling you the story, I am feeling mad at the bind I was in, but also mad at myself because I didn't handle her problems gracefully."

"Are you kidding me?" I said. "You should hear yourself! Think about what you *did* for her, not what you *didn't* do."

"Thanks. I appreciate that. I guess what I am saying is that, during the entire time with her, I felt like a tea kettle with the top glued on, ready to blow. I resented feeling that I was being taken for granted. I don't want to feel that way. I want to care for people and not resent them for needing me."

"Someone said, 'The good you do today, people will often forget tomorrow; do good anyway.'"

"I know. I have heard that, too, and I swear I am working on it," she said, "because most of my clients will forget before tomorrow."

I nodded and smiled. "You said that after this experience you know what you would do if you were God."

"I'd do two things." She paused. "First, I would send all caregivers in the world lower expectations for recognition plus unlimited helpings of patience."

"And the second?"

"I would inspire someone to invent a decent hospital gown."

In This Together

"When we say anyone can succeed if they work hard enough—it's all relative. How often do you hear a poor person say anyone can succeed?"

David is a successful, independent financial manager. I have known him for many years and watched him start and grow his business. His story is about hard work, the nature of success, and the luck of the draw.

David began his business career following his dad in banking. After ten years working as a loan officer, then a vice president, he struck out on his own to become a private money manager. Getting started wasn't easy. Many times he wondered if he had done the right thing quitting his steady job. Now, by himself, David manages an impressive amount of his clients' money and produces exceptional returns.

You might expect him to be a conservative thinker, and he is when it comes to managing money. In his personal life, however, he is a passionate liberal. I told him about my book, and I explained my theory about dreaming the impossible to discover the less impossible. Then I asked him what he would do if he could be God. He took a few days to think about it, then we got together at his office, and he told me his ideas.

"What concerns me most is the growing gap between rich and poor," he began. "Most of my clients come from good families, a few from old money. They are intelligent, educated, and they are able to imagine their futures. They also had a lot of help. Contrast that with being born as a minority in the inner city, or trying to find work as a migrant laborer coming from Mexico or Central America."

"So, if you could be God, what would you do about it?"

"I know this will sound naive, but you asked me to step outside my lifebox. So this is what I would do. I'd take all of the people who have had the breaks and the support to help them succeed, and I would swap their lives with people who never had opportunities or help, but who work their asses off just to stay afloat."

"What would that achieve?"

"Empathy. It would teach the wealthy how hard it is to succeed in this world when you are born poor. People who live in gated communities are cloistered from relationships with the poor. They have no way to feel the desperation of not being able to pay the rent. Even the middle class have no idea what it's like to live on the streets, or in a shelter. The wealthy don't ride the bus to work, or walk to work, or even worry about work. They worry about losing their wealth.

"The definition of success for people who live at the poverty level—and that includes forty million people according to the latest numbers—is a high school education. Very few can afford anything beyond that, including a community college education, let alone a four-year one. Poor people don't have the necessary connections to get into an Ivy League school—or because of what it costs today—even a state university."

"Would this life switch be permanent?"

"No, but I would make them believe it was; otherwise, it wouldn't have much effect. I am not out to punish people. I just want people of means to know what it's like to struggle. You can learn empathy by walking a mile in someone's shoes, but all that means to some people is that you are now a mile away and have a new pair of shoes. Becoming suddenly poor is only instructive if you feel trapped."

"What about people who succeeded from nothing? I know a lot of people who believe that success is possible for anyone who is willing to work hard enough. What do you think about that?"

"Barack Obama became President of the United States. That doesn't mean every black man—or for that matter, anyone—can become president. In the history of this country, that office has been held by only forty-four people, including Barack Obama. When we say anyone can succeed if they work hard enough—it's all relative. How often do you hear a poor person say anyone can succeed? Most poor people can't even imagine it. That's why President Obama is such a hero to so many people around the world."

"You said you aren't out to punish the rich for their success."

"No. I just want them to be reminded that success has a lot to do with the luck of the draw, not just hard work. The real wealth in this country has been passed down through generations. And it is highly concentrated. We have four hundred billionaires in this country. Did you know that?"

"I didn't."

"Eighty percent of the stock market value is owned by twenty percent of all investors. That concentration of wealth is dangerous to the future of this country."

"How so?"

"Too much power controlled by too few. You know the Golden Rule."

"He who owns the gold makes the rules."

"Precisely. Have you seen *Les Misérables*? Or read the Victor Hugo book?"

"I haven't read the book, but I've seen both the play and the film."

"Then you know the dangers posed by a concentration of wealth and power."

"Wasn't *Les Misérables* published *after* the French Revolution?"

"Yes, about ten years after, in 1862, but Hugo began writing it around 1832 because he deplored the trend he saw in France. The French Revolution happened in 1848, and the chaos opened the door for Napoleon to rise to power in 1852. Hugo lived in self-exile for seventeen years after Napoleon came to power. The French Revolution was caused in part by the disenfranchisement of the middle and lower classes. Only landholders were permitted to vote. The country was ruled by the financial aristocracy including bankers, stock exchange magnates, railroad barons, and landowners. Sound familiar?

"Alexis de Tocqueville, the French historian, wrote about the growing problem of inequality in France. He said, 'We are sleeping together in a volcano.' He predicted that the lower classes would erupt in revolt."

"And you're worried about that happening here?"

"It happens in every society that is out of socioeconomic balance. It's the so-called Arab Spring. The desire for economic equality is also burning in China. Natural ecosystems seek balance; so do human societies."

"I'd like you to go back to what you said about wealth being the luck of the draw."

"Most wealth is about being in the right place at the right time. It's about where you were born, the parents you got, or maybe a lucky investment your parents made. Your success could also result from a chance meeting at a party with someone who knows someone with influence who can help you. Friends take care of friends. But what if you don't have any influential friends?"

"You must have some clients who came from meager beginnings."

"Most of my clients are doctors and other professionals, and people with trust funds. The professionals made their money from hard work, but very few came from nothing. It takes money to pay for medical school, or law school, or to get any kind of college degree. I am willing to bet that luck was even more important for the ones that could raise themselves out of poverty."

"What kind of luck?"

"Exceptional intelligence or talent—or sitting on land that was worthless until a petroleum engineer invented fracking. If you were lucky enough to own land in the Bakken shale formation of North Dakota, you might receive royalties from the oil companies drilling for oil and gas on your otherwise worthless property. Who could have imagined that? If you own farmland and grow corn, who could have dreamed you would receive a government subsidy to produce corn to be used as an additive to gasoline? These things have nothing to do with your talents or hard work. It's the luck of the draw."

"But you started with nothing and now you're successful. That wasn't luck."

"Sure it was. I had great parents, and a father who educated me about money. I was lucky to be born with a good mind, but I didn't earn my intelligence either. I'm a curious person. Maybe I was born with a curiosity gene. My parents definitely encouraged me to explore. We know that some people are better equipped to succeed. We are not all playing on the same field with the same equipment. IQ is also not a function of hard work."

"What about people with average IQs? Won't hard work help them succeed?"

"Of course. Bill Clinton reportedly has an IQ of about 140, and George Bush has an IQ of about 125. I don't know if these numbers are factual, but assuming they are true, it shows that IQ is not the only factor determining success. Whatever you think of their politics, both men had to work hard to reach the presidency, but one had a substantial head start.

"The average IQ in the U.S. is 100. Imagine how many folks are below 100 to make 100 the average. How does someone with an IQ of 70 compete with a 130? Nature is not fair. That's why we need to have empathy for people who are entering the human race twenty yards behind the starting line."

"How important is liking what you do?"

"Liking what you do is a huge factor in success. You and I may feel that we work harder than most people, but would you trade what you do for working on a numbing assembly line, or bent over on hands and knees thinning sugar beets, or picking lettuce, or stacking hay in a dusty barn, or unloading railroad cars by hand? It's very difficult for a poor person to make enough money to reach escape velocity to transcend their circumstances and enjoy the luxury of doing what they love."

"What about supply and demand? Isn't that how the marketplace works?"

"Sure, and there is a lot of luck involved in beating the market. Why should you get more of the pie because you are lucky? I know that works in the jungle, but we have evolved, haven't we?"

"What about lottery winners? Should they have to share their winnings with the rest of us? Didn't they take the risk?"

"Yes, but the government still takes our share for us."

"The lottery winner also shares his good fortune by buying things that other people make and need to sell. The money gets spread around naturally, doesn't it?"

"Of course," David said, "and the lottery winner is more proof that luck plays a role in success. Some neuroscientists also think ambition may be a function of hormones and brain chemistry. That's luck, too. But what if you are born without ambition, or have parents who don't care about you? When all is said and done, people do what they want, and some will make bad choices regardless of their opportunities. But if I were God, I would make sure that everyone had enough opportunity to overcome the bad luck of being born in the wrong country, to the wrong parents."

"That sounds like social engineering," I said. "I thought you were a Libertarian."

"I know my plan of swapping lives is an impossible idea. It just makes me feel better to think I am doing something to decrease contempt for people who don't have much. You are always talking about using the impossible to discover the less impossible."

"What is your less impossible?"

"Empathy. Less contempt for the poor. Do I need to say it again? I know it's impossible to swap lives, but it is less impossible to be concerned about our tax policy. If we empathize with the poor, we have a better chance of hearing them the next time someone brings up the minimum wage or health care."

"I'm sorry. I guess I don't know any well-off people who feel contempt for the poor."

"But you know people who think people are poor because they are lazy, or believe unemployment compensation discourages people from finding work. I'm sure in some cases it does, but some of my clients make it sound like being out of work and collecting an unemployment check is a vacation. In most states, these payments amount to less than half of what recipients were making in their jobs. Could you live on that? If you're working for minimum wage, and you get laid off because of what unscrupulous bankers did in New York, you collect half of your minimum wage. Would you willingly take a fifty percent pay cut? I couldn't. Would you trade places with somebody who couldn't find a job? What about health insurance? How would you pay the rent? What if your child needs a tooth pulled, or glasses, or non-generic medicine? The things we take for granted are monumental problems for poor people."

"I understand."

"I can't even imagine what twenty million unemployed people would do if they had no safety net. How would they live? Can you see the legions of beggars hanging out at freeways on the off-ramps? When we are hit with weather disasters, the victims need help, and we understand that. We don't blame them for the storms. But many people blame the poor because they think poverty is their fault. In most cases it is the luck of the draw, but people quote the exceptions to make a case that poor people are leeches on society, and it's not so."

"What about people who abuse the system? They could work, but would rather scam the welfare programs."

"The people who scam the welfare system are not your average poor people struggling to make ends meet. They are the professional thieves that know how to cheat on a massive scale. These criminals exist among the poor and the rich alike. Scam artists like Bernard Madoff and Charles Ponzi exist at every level of society."

"What about the two Boston Marathon bombers? Their family received all sorts of government assistance. Was that right?"

"That is such an isolated case, such an anomaly, that it isn't worth discussing. It's a sound bite used to stir up resentment for immigration policy and to tarnish programs that help immigrants settle in this country. Besides, who do you think profits most from that government assistance?"

"Who?"

"The merchants that provide goods and services."

"So, you're saying we are okay compensating victims of disasters, or investors who lose money, so why not the poor and immigrants?"

"Of course. The only real difference is that we feel justified compensating victims of natural disasters because we feel *empathy* for them. They own houses. We own houses. We belong to the same economic tribe. We can imagine ourselves needing similar support at some point. But we also pick and choose who receives aid based on their guilt or innocence."

"What do you mean?"

"Someone who buys a house on a hill may not readily empathize with someone who buys on the banks of a river, where there is a risk of flooding. Some people believe if you lose your job because of a bank meltdown or a merger, you should have been more careful about where you worked, or you should have seen disaster coming and stepped out of the way. If a tornado cuts a swath through your living room, you should have lived somewhere else. But the fact is, we are a society reliant on one another. We are all in this together, dependent on one another."

"How do you feel about paying higher taxes because of your empathy?"

"I hate taxes, but given the choice between landing in the highest tax bracket or the lowest, I'll take the highest."

"You care to explain that?"

"If I'm paying a lot of taxes, it means I'm making a lot of money."

"You earned that money, too. You worked hard, educated

yourself, took a risk leaving a safe job. You sacrificed to get where you are. You are a self-made man. Why shouldn't you reap the full reward?"

"Self-made? No such thing. The cream rises to the top is another cliché. Where would the cream be without the milk to support it? Don't let anyone kid you. We all stand on the shoulders of those who came before us and struggle beside us. We are all in this together. That's why I mentioned *Les Misérables*. It reminds us that no society can survive for long if the rich eat the cake and the poor only get the crumbs."

Now What's Wrong?

"I have been shopping at Ralphs for years, ever since they set up their club program, so why didn't my number work?"

Friday morning was the time for trash pickup in our old neighborhood. I used to retrieve the empty cans around noon. That was about the only time I saw my neighbor Harry. One day he was also collecting his empties, and I waved to him. He held up his hand, signaling for me to stay where I was. He hurried over to me.

Harry likes to get in your face when he talks. A couple of feet away is close enough for me, but he stands almost nose to nose. When he goes off on something, he also spits, making a conversation feel like an unwelcome dance. I back up and he glides forward. This used to bother me until Mary Lou told me he is hard of hearing. I suppose that is an explanation, if not an excuse, but I wish he would invest in hearing aids so I could engage him rather than just listening to him complain.

"Have you had any trouble lately with the cable company?" Harry asked me. He never asks if you have a minute to talk. He just starts in.

"What kind of trouble?" I asked, practically shouting.

"With your DVR! I just had a nasty phone conversation with customer service. My DVR isn't working. My kids are coming tomorrow for the weekend, and my grandson wants to watch football. All of a sudden I can't get a picture. I know it's the DVR. Everything runs off it. The woman I talked to told me they could send out a technician next week. I told her that's too late, but she said it was the best she could do. I reminded her I have been a loyal customer for ten years. She had my account right there in front of her on the computer, so she knew I paid my bill every month. I reminded her that I could switch to Direct TV. 'When you need me,' I said, 'I pay the bill. When I need you, I get zip. Why is that? Do you want to lose me as a customer? I'm sure Direct TV would love to have my business.'"

While he talked, I was thinking about my own digital recorder. I know they are prone to bugs that seem to show up during my favorite program or a big game. Time Warner, our cable provider, does a good job for us. Harry, on the other hand, lived a few doors down and seemed to have a lot of trouble.

At one time in my life, I was constantly dividing the world into two kinds of people. I guess I was trying to make sense of life. Categorizing felt comfortable, if not meaningful. Anyway, I would say things like, "The world is divided into two kinds of people: those who should have kids and those who shouldn't," or "those who complain about everything and those who don't." Harry is a chronic complainer.

"Harry," I said, "I have an extra DVR in our guest bedroom. We won't need it over the holidays. You are welcome to it."

"I don't want to put you out."

"It's no problem. I can get it right now."

"No, I have no idea how to connect it. I have this hi-tech system the Geek Squad put together. I don't know what they did. You will never figure it out, either. That's why I wanted a cable guy to come out and bring a new box. He should set it up; unless he's like the idiot they sent last time."

"You're right," I interrupted. "I shouldn't mess with your system."

Harry went on, "They told me I could drive to one of their offices and pick up a new box, but why should I have to do that? I pay for service. I want service. Don't you think that's right?"

"I do appreciate good service," I said.

"Besides, I don't like to drive with all of the traffic on the streets during the holidays. I went to the market yesterday, and I couldn't believe the cars. I got cut off by this kid and almost ran into the median. I'm sure he was texting. People drive too fast on that street. The speed limit should be thirty miles per hour, not forty-five. Don't you agree?"

"I haven't really had a problem."

I don't think he even heard my reply. He kept on without skipping a beat. "And the clerks in that store are impossible to deal with. The lines are too long, and they won't open another register. I can't believe how much garbage people pile into their baskets. That's why we have such a problem with obesity and diabetes in this country. I can't understand all the junk. I finally got up to pay, and I gave them my club number so the little Mexican checker would give me my discount. She said the number was not in the system. I told her I wanted to talk to the manager. She said he was on break, but I told her I wasn't moving until she gave me my club discount. Then she left to find the manager. She came back and instead of her telling him the problem, she wanted me to explain it to him. I felt like I was in the hospital. You have to repeat your story to everyone that comes in to look at you. You ever been in the hospital?"

I nodded.

"They were supposed to enter all of our health information on a computer."

"Was the line of shoppers behind you stacking up?"

"What?"

"Were people in line behind you getting angry . . . while you were waiting for the manager?"

"I don't know, why?"

I let that go. "What happened with the manager?"

"The manager! I told him my wife and I have been shopping at Ralphs for years, ever since they set up their club program, so why didn't my number work? It's the damn computers. Or it's that clerk. She didn't enter it right. I don't carry a card around with me. My wife has the card. I told him to look her up. Then he tells me I'm not at Ralphs; I'm at Albertsons."

Harry shakes his head and throws his arms in the air. "Of course my club number won't work at Albertsons if it's a Ralphs number. Why couldn't they have told me that in the first place instead of wasting my time? Nobody pays attention anymore."

He looked down at my trash can and said, "Where did you get that?"

"Home Depot."

"Home Depot? I hate that place. I tried to buy a trash barrel with a lid attached, and they said that size doesn't come that way. But yours is attached. So they lied. They do sell them with attached lids."

"No, I attached the lid myself with some plastic ties. Look. The lids have little holes already punched in. Just run the twist ties through the holes and around the handle on the can. They won't get separated and lost when the wind blows the whole thing down the street. In fact, when the lid hangs off the side, it won't roll at all."

"Well, you see. Why didn't they tell me that?"

"I don't know, Harry." About then I was not in the mood to listen to more of his complaining. I thought maybe I could encourage him to be more positive. I told him I was working on a new book, and I asked him what he would do if he could be God.

"I don't believe in God," he said. "It's a bunch of crap!"

"That's okay. Just pretend you have unlimited power. What would you do? What would you change?"

"Don't get me started."

"Pick one thing. What one thing would you do to change the world for the better?"

He thought for a moment. Then he said, "Tolerance! I think this world would be a damn lot better off if people were more tolerant."

Secrets

"Of course God has a point of view. Why else do you think he made humans? He likes to watch us fall crazy in love."

Liz is what marketers call an experiential, meaning she wants to experience life to the fullest. She's twenty-six and likes to skydive, teach yoga, travel the world, and generally chase life. She is also in love with Tim, her boyfriend of three years. Liz told us Tim wants to get married and raise a family. She has more life to experience and doesn't want to be tied down.

Mary Lou and I were sitting with her in an outdoor cafe, talking about her love dilemma. I thought I might shake things up a little by asking her what she would do about her choices if she were God.

"God? How would that make a difference?"

"Maybe thinking about it from a different perspective will open you to more possibilities. You could turn Tim into your fellow traveler. He could live an adventurous life along with you instead of hoping you will settle down with him in Chicago. Imagining that you have the power to do anything may help you find a solution."

She shook her head. "I couldn't manipulate Tim. I respect that he loves Chicago."

"What do you love?"

"I want to move to Brazil and teach yoga."

"But, you also love Tim. You said you have been playing this cat and mouse game for three years."

"It's not a game. We are two different people, that's all. But I still love him just the way he is."

"Why don't you break it off and go separate ways?"

"We can't. I can't."

"So you want to eat your cake and have it, too. But you don't like how this current cake tastes. Maybe you would be more satisfied if you gave Tim the cake and moved on."

Liz picked up her fork and just stared at me without answering. I was a little worried about what she might do with the fork. I was trying to motivate her to consider the impossible, but she wasn't picking up on it.

"Have you told him all of this?" Mary Lou said.

"Not exactly."

"After three years together, he doesn't know what you want?"

"He knows I don't want to live in Chicago."

"How about kids?"

"I haven't told him that I don't want kids."

Mary Lou and I looked at each other with amazement. I asked her, "Why haven't you told him?"

"Because I'm hoping I will change after I've had a chance to experience life."

Mary Lou waded in, "That's a lot of anxiety to carry."

"I would rather live with the anxiety than lose him."

"What about Tim?" Mary Lou said. "Maybe he doesn't want to live with the anxiety anymore. It sounds like you want him to make a choice for you. If he says he's moving on, how will you feel?"

She put the fork down and I breathed easier. She carefully folded her napkin and set it aside. "I have to use the ladies' room."

She rose from the table and headed off. I motioned for the waiter to bring us more coffee. While we waited for Liz to return, we talked about when we were dating and felt pulled in different directions.

"She's right," Mary Lou said. "If she changed Tim into someone like herself, she may not find him attractive anymore. Maybe they are drawn to each other because they are different. He is an accountant. You can't get much different than that—I mean compared to her. I think there is a lot to the theory that we pick our partners to complete ourselves."

I said, "I was just curious about what she could do if she looked at her choices through a wider lens, a different filter. Being God is just a metaphorical way of feeling the power to think differently. It never hurts to try another point of view."

"Does God have a point of view?"

"Of course God has a point of view. Why else do you think he made humans? He likes to watch us fall crazy in love."

Mary Lou laughed and took my hand.

Liz returned. She sat down and looked at Mary Lou, then at me. "You guys seem so well-suited for each other. Was it easy for you to settle down and get married?"

Mary Lou and I looked at each other and smiled. In unison, almost in pure harmony, we said, "We dated for three years."

"I didn't know that." Liz sat up in her chair, looking eager for more information. "So there is hope for Tim and me?"

"I think three years is the breaking point," I said. "Or," I added, "in the case of love, we could call it the breakup point."

Mary Lou had a slightly different take. "Three years is actually about a year past my breakup point. I was ready to move on when he proposed. I never thought it would happen. I wasn't going to wait any longer."

Liz smiled and then her face lit up. "I know!" She looked like she had discovered diamonds. "I know what I would do if I were God!"

"Great!" I said.

"You said your breakup point was three years. If I were God, I would extend my breakup point to four years. Maybe by then I will want to have kids. I think I just need Tim to wait a little longer."

"Why don't you tell Tim how you feel?"

"Because he wants three kids. What if I tell him I don't, and he decides to look for someone else?"

I said, "And what if he says he understands and is willing to wait until you are ready?"

"I can't take that chance. And I can't promise him I will ever be ready."

Mary Lou said, "If you don't tell him what's holding you back, he may think you don't love him."

"He knows."

"Are you sure?" I said.

"Positive."

"Then why are you afraid he won't understand that you don't want kids?"

She didn't answer right away. She took a drink of coffee and slowly set the cup down. She took a deep breath. "Maybe I am afraid."

"Of what?" I said.

In a quiet voice she said, "That he doesn't love me enough to wait."

No one spoke for a few moments.

Finally I said, "Wouldn't it be a relief to find out one way or the other?"

"I don't know," Liz said.

Mary Lou said, "Why did you want to meet with us today?"

"Because I want to know your secret."

We looked at each other as if to say, do we have a secret? Then Mary Lou said, "Our secret is that we don't try to guess what each other is thinking. We talk about our fears and worries. We are honest with each other, knowing that our love is strong enough to deal with it."

I said, "When you put your head on the pillow each night, wouldn't it be better to know that your secrets aren't holding you hostage?"

Liz looked at us. Tears welled up in her eyes and staggered down her cheeks. She blotted the tears with her napkin and didn't talk about her feelings after that. We talked about nothing important for a few minutes, then we paid, hugged, and said goodbye, wondering how it would all work out.

Two days later Liz called. Mary Lou answered the phone and motioned for me to get on the extension. Liz sounded excited, happy. She told us she had decided to move to Brazil for one year. Mary Lou asked her what had happened with Tim. Liz said she told him how she was feeling, why she was holding back.

"I confessed my feelings about not wanting kids . . . and told him I wanted to go to Brazil."

"And?"

"And he asked me if there was room for two Americans in Brazil."

"Does that mean he wants to go with you?" I asked.

She squealed with excitement. "Yes! He said he wanted to experience what I wanted to experience. He said kids can wait, but his love can't."

"That's wonderful!"

"I'm going down to find us a place. He is quitting his firm. I thought he loved accounting, but he said as long as we were being honest about what we wanted, he had a secret to reveal to me. He's always wanted to write a novel, but he was worried I would think he wasn't serious about us. I never knew that he wanted to write."

"So it sounds like everything is great."

"I can't thank you guys enough. I kept thinking about what you said about hiding secrets when I went to bed. I don't want to feel like I'm hiding something . . . and you asked me that question about what I would do if I could be God."

"Uh-huh."

"At the time I thought it was a bizarre question. I didn't understand what you were saying. Then I realized if I were God, I wouldn't be afraid of anything. I wouldn't be afraid to tell the truth or know the truth. It made me feel powerful. I think it gave me the confidence to accept whatever might happen. I just didn't want to live with a lie."

"I'm glad it worked out," I said. "I have a question for you."

"Okay."

"I don't want to throw cold water on what happened, but I am curious. What if Tim had not understood?"

She paused a moment before answering. "I thought all night about that possibility. I decided that it wouldn't be fair to Tim if I didn't tell him what is in my heart. I prepared myself for the worst. I know life is not a fairy tale. But however it works out for us, I want it to be fair."

Miss Direction

"Ben looked like he was about to tackle her as she pranced off like one of those Victoria's Secret Angels. But she was no angel."

Ben is a volunteer high school football coach. Mary Lou and I have known him and his wife, Carol, for some years. They don't have any kids, so Ben's coaching is a big part of his life. He is a civil engineer, and he loves deciding how things are done. Ben says when he was eight, his dad asked him what he wanted to be when he grew up. He said he wasn't sure, but he knew he wanted a pointing job. His father asked him to explain what he meant by a pointing job. He answered it was a job where he pointed where to dig the hole, and somebody else dug.

Ben, the football coach, engineer—and pointer— is a born pedantic. He naturally needs to instruct people, to point out what they need to do in any situation. And he is especially good at instructing Carol. It is obvious, nevertheless, that they love and know each other well and have settled into their compatible roles—at least that's what we thought until we heard their story about buying a car.

We were sitting on the couch in their family room and

watching a video of Ben's recent football game. Ben was into the game as if he was standing on the 50-yard line calling plays to his quarterback.

When Ben's sophomore running back fumbled on their opponent's 10-yard line, he abruptly paused the video and turned to Carol and said. "Now you see, when you are in this situation, you need to cover up, wrap both hands around the ball."

"I know, honey." Carol nodded and went back to her knitting.

Ben looked at Mary Lou and me like we were on his staff, and we nodded as if to say, we got it coach!

Ben turned back to the TV and continued studying the game. Two minutes later he paused the video again and turned to Carol. "Now, when you are in this situation, you can't let them out of the hole. We can turn the fumble into a positive if we play it right. Do you see?"

"Yes, sweetheart, I see. You have them backed up to the ten, and if you hold them and they have to punt, you will have good field position again."

Ben nodded, "But here's where you need to watch for a misdirection play."

She looked at us and shook her head. "That reminds me of last week when we were buying a car."

Mary Lou said to Carol, "You got a new car?"

Carol nodded. "We had quite an experience. We were at the Honda dealer and Ben was coaching me on buying a car—even though I once worked at a dealership in the finance department and know pretty much everything about the strategies involved.

My problem is I hate the whole experience. So anyway, this young salesgirl came over to help us. She's in her late twenties, blonde, wearing a deliberately low-cut top, plenty of cleavage. In football, she is what Ben would call a misdirection play. So I dubbed her Miss Direction."

I said, "What happened, Ben?"

Ben turned toward us. "What happened to what?"

Mary Lou said, "To Miss Direction and you at the Honda dealer."

Carol said to Ben, "The salesgirl at the auto dealership." Ben shrugged. Carol went on, "Miss Direction led us to one of those little offices and asked us if she could get us something to drink. She only looked at Ben when she asked. It's like I wasn't even there, even though she should have known that women are the ones who bless the purchase." She paused and looked over at Ben to see his reaction. He shrugged again and let her continue without interrupting.

"Ben said he would like some water. So Miss Direction excuses herself with a flourish and a cute baby smile—at my husband—and says she will be right back. She has him sitting where he can watch her bend over and pick up her purse, then walk away so he has a great view of her 'end zone'—if you get my drift. Ben looks like he's about to tackle her as she prances off like one of those Victoria's Secret Angels. But she was no angel. I didn't need to watch her. Watching Ben was more entertaining."

"I wasn't watching her," Ben said.

Carol raised an eyebrow at Ben, then she continued, "Anyway she comes back with Ben's water, and we start telling her what were looking for. It irritated me that she never looked at me when she talked."

"Did you get a good deal?" Mary Lou asked.

Carol said, "The base price looked okay, but then she started adding the extras. No matter what Miss Direction wanted to load onto the base price, Ben just nodded okay and said, 'We can do that.' But when she said we should probably upgrade the steering wheel, I had heard enough, and I told her we just wanted the basic model."

Now Ben explained his strategy to us, "I let 'em load me up. Then I tell 'em we don't want all of the extras, so they throw 'em in anyway."

Carol said to us, "You know how it works. They ask you how much you want the monthly payments to be. So I low-balled her at $199 per month. She says that sounds low, but they might be able to do something. She needs to clear it with her manager. I knew they couldn't do it at that price, but it's a game. They'll push it higher from wherever you start. And I know they have wiggle room on leases based on where they set the residual value."

Ben added, "And you know how women are expected to be unreasonable, so I just let her run with it." He laughed.

Carol returned a whatever-you-say-honey smile and went on with her story. "Anyway, Miss Direction leaves, and Ben asks me to tell him the max I'm willing to pay. I tell him $199. And he says, 'That's impossible. You'll never get it.'"

"We sat there for at least fifteen minutes," Ben said.

Carol added, "I know Miss Direction is waiting back in the sales lounge watching *Housewives of Beverly Hills* while we are supposed to be sweating bullets, praying we'll get our price.

She finally returns and says she fought for us and was even willing to drop her commission to make the deal work, but the boss won't go any lower than $299."

Ben said to Mary Lou, "I thought $299 was still a good price, but Carol just shakes her head, and you'll never guess what she says to the salesgirl."

Carol interrupted, "I said to her, 'If you could be God, would you give us this car at that price?'"

Then Carol turned to me and said, "Miss Direction looked at me the way I looked at you when you asked me that question. Anyway, I sat there, stone-faced, waiting for her answer. Ben looked at me like I had lost it. Miss Direction said that if she could be God, she'd give a free car to everyone. So I said, 'Sounds great. Present that offer to your boss.' She looked out the window like she was actually considering it. She was good. She knew I was working a little misdirection of my own, so she said she'd see what she could do for us."

Ben explained, "This time she comes back in about five minutes and says her boss approved $249, but we have to add $900 cash. I was thinking that we should take it, but Carol gets up and walks away without saying a word."

"What did you do?" I asked Ben.

"I went with her. Hell, I didn't know where she was going."

Carol said to me, "I thought the price was still pretty good, but you said that if you dream the impossible, it could lead to the less impossible."

Ben said, "I still thought she was dreaming. Now we are standing outside the building, waiting for the salesgirl to chase after us. Sure enough, here she comes. She says she has an idea.

So we go back inside."

"Long story short," said Carol, "we got it for $239 a month without having to increase our down payment."

"How did you work that?" Mary Lou asked.

Carol said, "I held out for the less impossible."

Ben shrugged.

Carol smiled and returned to her knitting, her slender fingers working away. Then she stopped for a moment and looked over at Mary Lou and me, then at Ben. She said, "Believing I have the power to face any challenge head-on is like going into a football game with a good plan and the confidence to carry it out. I hate buying cars with a passion, but all the time we were haggling, I kept telling myself to breathe, relax, and stay composed. I guess, in that sense, I was playing God."

I asked Ben how he felt about the car-buying experience.

Ben looked at Carol; then he spoke to us, "I gotta admit, Carol made me realize something. Lately I've had this defeatist attitude. She thinks it's because my team isn't playing well. We lost the last two games that we should have won. Now I'm wondering if the reason we're losing is because my attitude is rubbing off on my players. We're playing the Palm Springs Indians next week. Last week I thought it would be impossible to beat them."

"But you don't think so this week?" Mary Lou asked.

"No. I think we have a chance."

"What's changed?" I asked.

"This week Carol will be on the sidelines with me."

Mary Lou said, "What is Carol going to do?"

"She's going to remind me to coach like I'm God."

Ascot & Red

Red said, "He's not asking you, Satan. He wants to know what a normal person would do if she were God."

The annual Palm Springs International Film Festival is held in January. Hollywood stars attend in droves. Film lovers like Mary Lou and me can watch movies from all over the world. You wouldn't think it was much fun standing in long lines waiting to get into the theater, but we have met some interesting people in those lines.

One evening we were in line, and a couple standing behind us was talking about one of the films they viewed the night before.

"I liked it," the woman said. "Why didn't you?"

"It was just more religious propaganda."

"No, it wasn't. It was sweet."

"I suppose you liked *The Passion*, too," he said.

"I didn't see it," she answered.

This seemed like the perfect moment for me to step in. I turned around and inserted myself into their conversation. "Hey, I saw *The Passion*."

They both looked at me as if to say, why are you butting into our conversation? I was undeterred. "Can I ask you both a question?"

They glanced at each other. The young woman said, "You can ask me. He's in a bad mood."

She looked to be in her twenties. She had red hair and wore a mismatched combination of stripes and plaids that I actually liked. Her partner looked about the same age. He wore a little, brown Ascot cap, rimless glasses, and sported a Van Dyke mustache and goatee. I stereotyped him as a writer, maybe an artist. I addressed the young woman. "I couldn't help overhearing your conversation. I am writing a book, and I was wondering if you could help me by answering a question."

She shrugged. "Okay."

"I'd like to know what you would do if you could be God."

The guy piped in, "I'm an atheist!"

She turned to him—I'll call her Red—and she said, "That's not true! You don't know what you are."

"That's okay," I said. "You can be whatever you want. But how would you answer the question? What would you do if you could be God?"

The guy—I'll call him Ascot—said, "The question is irrelevant. If there is no God, how can I imagine what I would do?"

Red said, "He's not asking you, Satan. He wants to know what a normal person would do if *she* were God."

Ascot said, "If there was a God, *he* would not care what you do."

Again, I asked Red, "So what would you do?"

Red looked at Ascot with a stare equal to a heavyweight punch. He held up his hands with palms toward her as if warding off her blow. She turned to address me. All this time Mary Lou is poking me in the ribs, whispering for me to leave them alone. But this was far too interesting for me to bow out now.

Red looked at Mary Lou, then at me. Now Mary Lou also seemed curious about what Red was about to say. She leaned forward to hear.

"If I were God, I would make a movie about myself for the people who don't believe in me," she said, nodding with her whole body.

Ascot interrupted. "She's a painter. She said that because she thinks nobody believes in her."

"I'm talking about God, not me," Red interjected.

"Really?" I said to Ascot. "Do you believe in her?"

"Of course!" he snapped, as if it should be obvious.

Red turned to Ascot. Her face brightened. "You really believe in me?" She said it like this was a revelation.

He took her hands and said loudly enough for us to hear, "You are the only thing in this world that I believe in."

Their feisty battle turned soft and caring. Mary Lou clutched my hand, and we turned around to give them their moment. I thought about what fragile creatures we are, and how much more possible it is to believe in ourselves when someone we love confirms our worth.

The movie we saw that night was good, but I will always remember Ascot and Red. Their two-minute scene outside the theater was worth the price of admission.

The Emancipator

"It takes courage to quit some things. So get out there and quit what isn't working. Then go fail at something. It will give you courage."

One day I was using my iPad to check the latest box office numbers for movies opening that weekend. I'm interested because I love movies, and I am curious about trends. I was sitting on the couch, enjoying a cup of coffee, when I got a call from Darren, a friend I hadn't talked to in months.

After catching him up on what was going on with my family, I asked him about his wife Janet and their two boys. Instead of answering, he said that one of our mutual friends had mentioned my book, and he wanted to talk about it.

He began, "I have given this a lot of thought, and I am prepared to tell you what I would do if I could play God."

"Great! Let's hear it."

"Do you have time to listen? I hope I'm not interrupting anything."

"I'm all ears."

"Did you see Spielberg's movie about Lincoln?"

"Yes. I loved it."

"Well, here's the thing. Around the time it was released, I noticed a bunch of news stories about the Emancipation Proclamation. I know you are a fan of President Lincoln. Did you know he signed it on December 31, 1862, making New Year's Eve 2012 the sesquicentennial—the 150th anniversary of the signing? I'm quite sure God had no use for slavery and was no doubt pleased when Lincoln ended it."

"Uh-huh."

"Lincoln did what he could in 1862 as Commander-in-Chief of the Union. But he knew the question of slavery had to be settled once and for all. The Emancipation Proclamation was not a law; it was an executive order that applied only to the states that had seceded from the Union. He could invoke martial law in those states because they were in rebellion from the Union. The Emancipation Proclamation didn't apply to states that remained loyal to the Union. In fact, slavery was still technically legal in the states that remained in the Union, and it continued to be so until the passage of the Thirteenth Amendment three years later. But the point I was going to make is that the sesquicentennial made me think about other forms of emancipation."

"Such as… ?"

"Something that will affect all people regardless of their sex, color, age, or national origin."

"Okay…"

He paused a moment, then he said, "If I could be God, I would emancipate the human mind."

"Emancipate it from what?"

"From fear, from prejudice, from superstition, and even

from anxiety, guilt, and hatred. I think that would change the world, don't you?"

"Definitely."

"I'm talking about freeing your mind from fear to give you confidence to achieve. So you won't be afraid of failure."

"Are you speaking rhetorically, or because you think I'm afraid of failure?"

"Most people are."

"Why do you think that?"

"Because it's natural. But I think we would all be happier if we weren't so afraid to risk."

"Tell me more."

"Okay, here is an example. You are always worried that nobody will buy your next product or book. Think about all the things you could accomplish if fear didn't hold you back."

I didn't feel that anything was holding me back, but I didn't interrupt him.

He continued, "The Emancipation Proclamation is a perfect example of my point. Lincoln could have feared losing reelection. Instead he acted like God, and he changed the course of history. His proclamation was a bold move, and it set the table for the passage of the Thirteenth Amendment that freed four million slaves. He was the modern day equivalent of Moses."

I answered, "But if you were a slave, it wasn't that simple. Living free is no doubt better than living as a slave, but freedom in 1862 came at a high price. Tens of thousands of slaves died because of the war, precisely because they were granted freedom."

Darren countered, "I understand, but overcoming fear

means accepting responsibility for your life and your choices. My point is, we can be also be enslaved by our fears. Fearing the outcome can prevent us from pursuing our dreams."

"Fear also has a purpose," I said. "The fear of being burned keeps you from touching a hot stove. The fear of dying keeps you from leaping off a cliff. The fear of losing your life savings deters you from making risky investments. The fear of getting cancer can stop you from smoking. So fear can also be a good thing."

He fell silent. I inferred from his silence that something was wrong. "You okay?" I asked.

"I'm fine!" he said. But I could tell he wasn't. His voice sounded off. He was trying to convince himself that I was afraid of something. I wondered if he was projecting a fear of his own.

After a few more moments of silence, he said, "Aren't you ever afraid?"

"Of course. I was just trying to distinguish between worry and fear, and also to show that fear has a purpose . . . you okay?"

"I'm fine."

"You don't sound fine."

"Why do you say that?"

"For one thing, you haven't said a word about Janet. The last time we talked, you said you guys were arguing a lot. What's going on?"

"Nothing."

More silence.

I said. "Doesn't sound like nothing."

Finally he said, "If Mary Lou said she was leaving you, what would you do?"

"What are you talking about?"

Another long silence. I waited.

"Janet took the kids and went to her mother's."

Now I was beginning to understand the real reason he called. "Tell me what's going on."

We talked for an hour about what was worrying him and what had happened with Janet. I listened and asked questions. I didn't want to criticize Janet. She was a friend, too.

"It's not easy," he said. "She doesn't believe in me. Hell, I don't believe in me. I hate my job. I want to start my own business, but I'm afraid I won't make it. She says all I do is complain, and she's right. Now I'm afraid of what will happen if I can't see the kids."

"I understand. But when you called me, you said you were going to emancipate the world from fear."

"What a stupid idea! You must think I'm totally losing it."

"You said if you could be God, that's what you would do."

"But I'm not God. I'm nothing."

"You think that's how your friends see you?"

He didn't answer. So I said, "If you could be God, would you look down at you and see nothing?"

"I have no idea."

"Okay. That's a start."

"What does that mean?" he said now sounding defensive.

"If you are nothing, and have no ideas, you are a blank slate. You can think and become whatever you want."

He backed off. "What do I want? Please tell me."

"You want to be the Great Emancipator."

He let out a sigh of defeat, then he said. "But I'm not; I'm the Great Loser."

I waited trying to think of something more to say. Then I recalled reading some facts about Lincoln. "Why do you admire Lincoln so much?"

"Because he wasn't afraid to do what needed to be done."

"Where do you think he got his strength?"

"I wish I knew."

"I'll tell you. He got his strength from failure."

"Failure?"

"Lincoln was born into poverty. He lost something like eight elections before winning the Illinois Senate seat. He twice failed in business, and he suffered a nervous breakdown. Yet every failure made him stronger. His resilience made him the man he was, able to take on the enormous challenge of the presidency in one of the most pivotal times in American history. In my own experience, I've learned a lot from success, but the lessons from failure burned deeper and lasted longer. I've failed more times than I can remember, and each failure taught me something that led to future success. If you aren't failing, you aren't trying or challenging yourself. Failure will make you better if you use it. That's why I don't fear failure."

"Do you think I'm a quitter?"

"Why would I think that?"

"I want to quit my job."

"I don't equate quitting with failure. If I quit smoking, I would consider it a success. If I quit doing something that is hurting me, I'd consider it a success. If I quit a job that was tearing me up inside, I would consider that a success. It takes courage to quit some things. So get out there and quit what isn't working. Then go fail at something. It will give you courage."

"I already failed with Janet. That hasn't given me any courage."

"What did you learn from that failure?"

"She said I am too critical and controlling. She said I'm too angry to live with."

"What are you going to do with that knowledge?"

"Do you think I'm angry and controlling?"

"It doesn't matter what I think. What matters is what she thinks. I'll ask you again. If you could be God, if you could change anything in your life, what would you do?"

He didn't speak. I wondered if my advice was helping or hurting.

Finally, after a full minute of silence, he said, "If I could be God, I would change myself. I would quit trying to control everything. I would get some balls and quit the job I hate. And I would show Janet I can change."

"Good for you!" I said. "Call me back when you've made it happen."

I didn't hear from Darren again for three weeks. I wanted to call but decided to wait and see if he did change. Then one Sunday afternoon he called and we talked again. He sounded like a different man.

"I wanted to tell you that I quit my job."

"How does it feel?"

He laughed. "I feel emancipated!"

"You sound different."

"I feel different."

"What are you going to do?" I said.

"I have always wanted to open my own fishing gear shop, so I got a job at the Fishing Rod, a small store a few miles from home. I started last week and I love it. I am learning so much that will help me build my own place."

"That's great, Darren. How's it going with Janet?"

"I told her I quit my job. She actually congratulated me. She said it was a bold move—just what I needed."

"Any chance you are getting back together?"

"One thing at a time. I'm going to see her for a drink next week. Alone without the kids. Like a date."

"You sound happy."

"I am. Thanks, man. If you hadn't asked me that crazy question about being God, I would still be sitting in my office staring out the window. That question changed my life."

The Atheist

*She stopped for a moment, then she said,
"I don't need to be saved.
I need to feel loved."*

What do you think an atheist would say if given a chance to play God? I talked a lot about the nature of God with my friend Alison from Dallas, but I wanted to hear from someone who didn't believe in any God at all.

A friend gave me the name and phone number of someone he thought might offer me a unique perspective. Her name is Caitlin. I called her and discovered that she lives not far from me. I described my book to her, and she agreed to meet me at the Old Town Coffee Shop in La Quinta to talk about God, or about atheism. Either way I hoped for a lively conversation.

It's a small place, so I found her without any trouble. She looked just as she had described herself—five-five, curly black hair, red vest, tan pants. We sat at one of the high tables against the wall. I sprang for the coffee and we got acquainted, sharing thoughts about our families and how we came to live in La Quinta, California, also known as the "Gem of the Desert."

Once we felt comfortable with each other, I asked her if she would mind if I recorded our conversation. I hadn't done this before, but I wanted to be sure I quoted her correctly. After she agreed, I asked her if she had thought about what she would do if she could be God.

"Oh my!" she said in a firm, articulate voice. "What a conundrum! Not only do I not believe in God, but here you are offering me—a woman—the opportunity of a lifetime. A female God! How can I pass that up?" Her hint of a smile reflected the irony in her voice.

"Don't worry, it's purely hypothetical," I said, smiling back.

"Thank God! Or I guess I should thank myself, huh?" Now she smiled with her whole face.

I smiled back. "So, if you could be God, what would you do?"

"Okay, before I go into that, I have something specific to clear up about my atheism. Just mine. This is about my feelings."

"Fine. That's why I wanted to talk with you."

"Then let me begin by asking you a question."

"Okay."

"Would you agree that Christians believe God gave us free will?"

I nodded, wondering if she was a lawyer. I had been in court before and worked with a lot of lawyers. Her questioning technique was commonly used to set up a witness. So I asked her if she was a lawyer.

She blinked. "As a matter of fact, I am. How did you know? Did you Google me?"

"No." I told her a little about my legal experience. "Sorry for the sidebar. Go ahead."

"Here is my point. Do you think atheists should spend

eternity in Hell for *not lying* about their beliefs?"

"I'll need you to explain that."

"Imagine you are a game show contestant. Behind door number one is, 'I believe in God.' Behind door number two is, 'I don't believe in God.' You have free will to choose either door, but . . . if you choose door number two, you'll go directly to Hell. How is that 'free will' when there is only one possible right choice?"

"Game shows are like that. Some doors have a new car behind them and some have a rubber chicken. You have to pick the right door to get the prize."

"Let me explain it this way. Christianity teaches that believing in Jesus Christ is the only path to Heaven. But I have free will to choose not to believe in Jesus. Why should I be punished for exercising my God-given free will? I'm not hurting anyone. If I don't believe, I shouldn't lie and say I do. That is hypocrisy—a sin—and I can't get into Heaven if I am a hypocrite. The Pharisees were hypocrites, and Jesus threw them out of the temple. What am I supposed to do? Does God want me to lie? And wouldn't he know if I was lying? How do I solve this double bind?"

"I see your point. I don't know the answer."

"Plus, I resent being coerced into believing Jesus is the Son of God. Christians preach that God is love. But where is that love? Or is love just the current marketing program?"

"What do you mean?"

"God hasn't always been about love. The Old Testament is filled with stories about a vengeful, insecure, malevolent God that needs constant reassurance and loyal obedience."

"For example?"

"Exodus, 32: 26-39."

"What is that?"

"I'll give you the gist of it. The first time Moses brought the Ten Commandments down the mountain, he saw the Israelites worshiping a golden calf. He was monumentally angry, so he asked all those who believed in the one true God to join him. He told those who joined him that the Lord God of Israel wanted them to go back and forth from one end of the camp to the other and kill all the nonbelievers—even their own brothers, friends, and neighbors. God's chosen ones killed three thousand people that day. Moses told them that God would give them a great blessing for their handiwork. Does that sound like a loving God?"

"How do we know God actually ordered Moses to do this?"

"Either God condoned what Moses did, or Moses is a liar, or the Bible is wrong. Take your pick, but you can't have it three ways. If God condoned the murders, then Moses and God are both murderers, and they violated their own Sixth Commandment, 'Thou shalt not murder.' On the other hand, if Moses is lying about God ordering the murders, how can you believe anything in the Bible?"

She went on, "I have defended schizophrenics who say God told them to kill. So you can understand why I have doubts about people who claim they talk to God. The Reverend Jim Jones, Charles Manson, and other cult leaders also come to mind. Cultures make their gods fit the times. The Old Testament message was toe the line or burn in Hell. Now we live in abundant times, so the message is God is loving and kind. We say that we are created in God's image, but it is obvious to me that we cast God in the image that meets our needs."

"I won't argue that our views of God have changed over the centuries."

"Here is another irony. Take the First Commandment, 'Thou shalt have no other Gods before me.' It shows that God is jealous. What kind of God is that? Are we supposed to emulate his jealousy in our own lives?"

I had no answer. I wanted to get off this subject and find out more about her personal history. "When did you stop believing in God?"

"When I realized I am a lesbian and not welcome."

Surprise! I'm sure I blinked at that revelation. It's not that I think you can look at someone and predict their sexuality. But obviously I had assumed she was heterosexual, or I would not have been surprised. Not that it matters, but it did take me aback. It also doubled my interest in her point of view. Now I wondered how being a lesbian affected her spiritual views. All I could think of to say was, "Tell me more."

She said, "As much as I tried to deny my sexuality when I was younger, I had to accept it as a fact when I was twenty-six. *Coming out* wasn't easy, especially fifteen years ago. The Church's current position is to treat homosexuals with respect and compassion, but they still refer to homosexuality as a 'disorder,' even though they know the research shows that homosexuality is neither a sickness nor a choice."

"Do you mean it's genetic?"

"Not exactly, but close. Studies show that homosexuality runs in families, so there must be a genetic component. Current research, however, hasn't found a specific gene to explain it. The latest theory suggests that homosexuality is caused by what are called epigenetic marks, or 'epi-marks,' which are chemical switches regulating how the genes for femininity and masculinity are expressed. The point is, it's not a choice. I can't control who I am attracted to anymore than you can."

She stopped and took a sip of coffee, then she continued. "The Catholic Church has said homosexuality itself is not a sin, because by definition sin requires conscious premeditation, and they know we don't choose our sexuality. Still, they argue that homosexual acts are sinful because acting on our natural desires *is* a choice. God is supposed to be all about love. If there is a God, why would he make me as I am, yet condemn me to never be able to express my love?"

"Did you become an atheist because you felt rejected by the Catholic Church?"

"It was the catalyst. It opened the door to more questions. Earlier I talked about free will and how the choices of getting into Heaven are rigged—not that I believe in Heaven or Hell—but the Church judges me unfit and demands that I repent. How can I repent something I don't feel is wrong and don't control? If the Pope is supposed to be God's voice on earth, how can I believe in God? Either God made me the way I am, or God makes mistakes, or God doesn't exist. I know who I am, and I didn't choose my sexuality; ergo, God does not exist. Or God is evil and sadistic like the God of Moses, in which case I want no part of that God anymore than I would any despot."

I had not heard these arguments, and I was fascinated. I decided if I ever needed a good lawyer I knew who to call. Her logic was hard for me to argue. Then again I am not a scholar. I wasn't there to argue, anyway; I was there to learn her point of view. "Let me ask you a question," I said. "Apart from the passage about Moses that you mentioned, what do you think about the Bible as a whole?"

"I think it is a collection of hearsay letters and ancient stories like the one from Exodus. But you have to understand how the Bible was created. If you studied U.S. history, you know that a lot of heated debate and compromise took place in writing the United States Constitution. Religious leaders during the Roman Emperor Constantine's time, around 320 AD, also fought like constitutional lawyers over what stories and letters should be included in the Bible. This was sort of like writing the Christian Constitution. In his day, Constantine was laying down church law to join together his divided empire. True believers, of course, think that all this wrangling was guided by the hand of God."

"But you don't believe that?"

"Some Christian theologians explain the process this way. They say that God is like a boss who dictates a letter to his secretary. She types it, but it is the boss's words. That's a cute analogy, but a ridiculous one."

"Why is it ridiculous?"

"First of all, the writing of the Bible continued for centuries after Constantine died. How many bosses and secretaries did God need to write this book? Why didn't he sit down with a monk and get the job done in a year, or five years? For that matter, why did God need a scribe at all?

"These books were written in three different languages

by forty different authors over a period of more than fifteen hundred years. Christ's apostles didn't actually write any of the letters that appear in the Bible. We don't even know if Mark, or Luke, or any of the so-called Twelve Apostles were even literate. The original copies of the Bible that Constantine ordered to be hand scribed are long gone, so we don't know what was in the original versions."

She stopped a moment and excused herself to use the restroom. She was gone for a few minutes, and when she returned, I asked, "Why do you think the Bible endures if it isn't true?"

"Aesop's Fables existed even before written language. Are they true because they endured? The Bible has lasted for the same reason that civil laws have lasted. Civilization depends on law. The Old Testament was written before we had secular codes. Early civilizations needed to codify the law of the land."

"Let me ask you this," I said. "I'm sure you know intelligent people who believe in God and attend church. What is wrong with them—in your eyes? How can you see what they can't see?"

"I don't think there is anything wrong with people who believe in God. I don't judge *their* faith. I could be wrong about what I believe. No one can prove that God does or doesn't exist. I don't deny that faith in a higher power gives billions of people a sense of hope, even though I think Heaven is a hollow promise. But you asked me why I am an atheist. Nothing makes me believe in God in the conventional way. I believe in man's laws because we accept that they were written by men and understand that they can and should be changed as needed to adapt to changing values, such as equal rights for all.

I said, "People say one of the Bible's strengths is that it doesn't change. The Word of God can't be amended. Its values are constant."

"Actually, the Bible has been amended countless times over the centuries. Do you know that more than one hundred different versions of the Bible exist? By the way, nowhere in the New Testament does Jesus say that homosexuality is wrong. Paul, or whoever used that pen name, writes about it in his epistles to the Romans and the Corinthians, but it's just his opinion. He never quoted Christ on homosexuality."

I said. "What about the parables? Do you think stories about Jesus curing the sick or walking on water are all fiction?"

"These stories were written more than a thousand years ago. The longer you tell a story, no matter how impossible it sounds, the more believable it becomes. As I said, Aesop's Fables have been around longer than the Bible, but that doesn't mean grasshoppers, ants, or pigs can actually talk or reason. Parables are fables, too. Just because we feel there is truth in the principles and morals laid out in these tales, it doesn't make them factual."

I said, "I must say, you are remarkably passionate about what you believe and don't believe."

"I would like to believe in God. I would give anything to have the faith that my grandmother had. But I don't." She paused and finished her coffee, then she continued, "I know that changing behavior can change one's self-concept. What really depresses me, though, is how Original Sin is used to oppress the mind and the heart. The Church makes people believe they are born sinners, and when that message is repeated often enough, it's destructive to the psyche." She stopped for a moment, then she said, "I don't need to be saved. I need to be loved."

I studied her face when she said that. Her eyes turned glassy and for a moment I thought she might cry. I don't think I have ever talked to anyone who was more passionate about their beliefs, or who had questioned them in such depth. I wanted to console her, somehow, but I still had a few questions, so I pressed on.

"It sounds like you have a problem with religion more than with God," I said.

She looked out the window for a moment, then she turned back to me and said, "Maybe I do, I don't know. Like I said, I would like to believe, but I don't have any faith. When I ask questions, I'm told that faith answers all things. Just believe and everything will fall in place. But I am trained to seek proof. I have too many facts and unanswered questions, too much reason in the way of faith."

When she took a breath, I offered to refill her coffee.

She shook her head. "Thanks, I'm fine, and I have to get going."

"Caitlin, I appreciate all of your time and thoughts. It helps me understand your point of view. But I'd like to get back to the big question. Do you have something specific that you would do if you could be God?"

She adjusted herself on the high stool and looked down at her cup for a moment. Then she looked back up at me and said, "I appreciate you listening to me ramble on. When you told me about your book on the phone, I was intrigued. I appreciate having a few days to think about it, to respect what you are doing. I hope you will print at least some of what I said in your book."

"I'll write it the way you said it." I held up the recorder.

"Thank you. I know God is important to many people. I respect that. I must say, however, that if God exists, I am disappointed that he hasn't offered any absolute, contemporary offer of proof. We need to hear from God—if he is there—because human beings are more divided and confused about God than at any point in history. So, if I were God, this is what I would do."

She suddenly peeked at her watch and looked surprised. "Excuse me, I just realized I'll be late for an appointment if I don't leave right now." She reached down for her purse on the floor and pulled it up. She set it on the table. "I prepared something for you to read. You can call me if you need more explanation."

She opened her purse and took out a sheet of paper. She unfolded it and handed it to me. Then she gave me a generous hug and said goodbye. I watched her walk away. When she was gone, I began to silently read what she had written on the creased paper.

If I Were God

If I were God, I would prove my existence by preparing a high-definition video explaining why I have been silent all of these years. I would tell the world what I like about the current state of affairs on earth, and what needs to change immediately. I would deliver my message via YouTube and Facebook, with auto translation so all people could hear me in their native languages and replay my message as often as necessary. Plus, I would auto insert every name subliminally in every form of communication so each person would know that I am speaking directly to them with no interpreters to edit my message.

I would simulcast by radio and TV. I would speak directly to the minds of the billion people who didn't have access to any form of media, and they would remember what I said perfectly and with no other interpretation.

I would create an incontrovertible and indestructible document to be kept on file in every home, like the Declaration of Independence or the Magna Carta, for all to read. I would also tell the people of the world that I see no reason to remain incommunicado or to perpetuate the mystery surrounding creation, or evolution, or my plan for the future. I would create a personal Facebook page, "friend" the world, and write a daily post to stay in touch.

No more vague parables, no Dead Sea Scrolls, no councils, no conventions, no hearsay. Everything will come straight from the source—me. Constant bickering over what I meant to say or do has distorted my most important message, which is simply to love one another and be kind to one another. I created this world for all to enjoy, not destroy, and especially not to use my name or intentions to hate or fight each other.

In closing, I want you all to know that I accept the blame for these many centuries of confusion. My silence has left you all in a sad state, suffering at a rate I never intended. I am sorry about that. I promise to do better. Thanks for watching and listening. From now on I will be in touch on a daily basis. That's it for now.

Warmest regards,
God

Author's Notes

"If you start dreaming above the clouds, you will have a lot more choices about where to stop on your way down to earth."

We all bring our own imaginations to stories, and we see the characters from our subjective points of view. I have always wished, however, that authors would say what their stories mean to them. So I have decided to do a little of it here.

My decision to use short stories to show how to unleash your imagination and inspire change may seem like an odd approach. I chose this way because I feel that asking you to use your imagination demands some imagination on my part.

In the introduction to this book, I said that these stories are based on situations and conversations I've had over time. One challenge in writing what some people call "faction" is creating verisimilitude, the process by which the reader gleans truth from fiction because the story reflects realistic aspects of life. In other words, a story doesn't need to be true to feel true or express truth.

Apart from entertaining you, the point of this book is to show you how to create options and opportunities that may not be obvious without shifting your point of view.

Playing God gives you a metaphorical license endowing you with unlimited power and resources to address the problems that concern you. From your perch in the clouds, you can dream with abandon, encouraging the impossible to lead you to discover the less impossible.

As I said in one of the stories, when you start dreaming above the clouds, you have a lot more choices about where to stop on your way down to earth.

Playing God is meant to stimulate a new state of mind, one that will kick-start the creative process and ultimately lead you to solutions that can make a positive difference in your life and perhaps the lives of others.

Why not simply ask, "If you could do anything with your life, what would you do?" Here is the reason.

In "All You Need To Know" (the last story in the third book of the complete series), Alison said she believes that because we can't see God, we created Jesus so we would have an image of God to relate to. We don't have to agree with Alison's view of God to know that she is right about one thing—our ability to embrace any idea is easier if we can "put a face on it." This is why a faceless corporation puts a picture of its CEO on the cover of its brochure. This is why many faiths relate to their prophets through concrete personalities such as Abraham, Muhammad, or Buddha.

We know that a picture is worth a thousand words, so the ability to picture yourself as God creates an image of power and virtue. Further into the story, Alison also said she imagined God as the sum of all virtues such as love, hope, charity, fairness, creativity, compassion etc. Feeling virtuous, raises your self-esteem, giving you the confidence and the permission to do things that you otherwise thought were beyond your abilities. Playing God also helps you visualize yourself stepping outside your lifebox and becoming who you want to be.

Understanding the difference between thinking outside the box and stepping outside your lifebox is important. Thinking outside the box is an idiom that goes as far back as 1912; it was popularized in the 1960's by management consultants who used it as a technique to teach creative problem solving. I used it myself in 1972 when I taught a graduate class called Living Space Awareness at the University of Maryland, College Park.

For anyone not familiar with this puzzle, the so-called box is formed by a series of nine dots placed equidistant from each other and arranged to form a square. The challenge is to connect all of the dots using only four straight lines without lifting the pen from the paper. This feat can only be achieved by extending two of the lines outside the confines of the nine dots—or box—hence, thinking outside the box.

Stepping outside your lifebox, however, is a different concept. I created it as a way for you to see yourself and your behavior more objectively. Here is how I intend it to be used.

First, you must accept one simple maxim—that we all build our own lifeboxes. (Yes, you can find exceptions but don't let them apply to you.) Maybe you built your box by trying to live a blueprint drawn by your parents, teachers, friends, or spouses. Maybe you built a box that you don't like anymore. Whatever the size and shape of your box, you built it. You can blame others or thank others for their roles in helping you construct the walls and the roof, but you are still the architect of your own box. The walls are yours, and they may represent safety, fear, or anything that prevents you from realizing your dreams. The walls surrounding your lifebox can be made of concrete a mile thick and a mile high and seem impenetrable. But you built them; therefore, you may tear them down. It may not be easy, but when the walls are gone, you will know what it is like to live freely and do things you never imagined possible.

Let me give you a few examples of how this process unfolded for characters in two of the stories. In the first story, Kevin wants to build a model of Heaven. He believes that people will become more considerate of one another if they can see that Heaven is real and attainable. His idea sounds absurd on its face. How would he ever raise the money to get the water rights or pass all of the environmental regulations? What a silly idea! The more you think about executing such craziness, the walls go up and get thicker and higher by the moment.

But crazy thinking can lead to less crazy thinking, such as Kevin's virtual Heaven. We have no idea how his brainstorm for "Visit Heaven Now" website will become a reality, but he said he had computer skills. Perhaps he will post his big idea on crowdfunding websites such as Indiegogo.com, or Fundable.com. How much money must he raise to make his virtual online Heaven possible for all of us to visit? Who knows? Maybe someday it could even become a theme park or the ultimate three-week vacation.

My point is that the question about what he could do if he were God changed his frame of mind, making it possible to imagine the impossible job of creating Heaven on earth. This allowed him to visualize the less impossible, the idea for a website that could become a forum for millions of people to explore their faith, and actually lead us all to become a little nicer to each other.

This story is also about resilience. Kevin humbled himself, offering to work for free, yet he was still open to new possibilities. He might have stayed on the grass under a tree forever, complaining about the economy, or how much he lost in the banking scandals, but when asked what he would do if he could play God, he saw an opportunity to step outside of his lifebox and dream. Then he didn't waste time grousing about how hard it is to build a website, or that he could never do it because he didn't have the money. He unleashed his imagination and went off to change his life.

It's difficult to see solutions to many of our most difficult problems because we are boxed in by self-imposed walls. It's often easier for us to tell our friends how to solve their problems. Our solutions may be wrong for them, but my point is that it is easier to see solutions from outside the box.

In the story, "Innocent Cries," I was sandwiched between two women on a plane from Los Angeles to New York. Seated to my left, was a young mother trying to soothe her son's innocent cries. Seated to my right, was Sister Mary Ignatius, a nun soothing the pain of innocent children in the jungles of Guatemala and other remote corners of the planet. From the personal to the global, these two women devoted themselves to the service of children.

To use a business metaphor, the young mother's devotion is focused an inch wide (on her son) and a mile deep (on his specific needs). Her commitment to one child is singular and intimate. Her reward is the pleasure of feeling her child's breath on her neck, sharing the rhythm of his heartbeat against her own, and believing that his future is unlimited.

Sister Mary's devotion runs a mile wide (helping many children) and an inch deep (limited to the time she has with them). Her energies are spread over countless children and their families. Her devotion is to humanity. She will never feel a child growing inside of her, but she will feel the joy of dedicating her life to improving the quality of life for scores of children.

I asked Sister Mary Ignatius what more she could do to achieve her mission if she had God's power. That question prompted her to step outside her lifebox and imagine raising the money needed to eradicate disease by selling the Vatican's assets. That was a huge leap of faith—an impossible idea—absolutely unimaginable. Yet, by playing God, Sister Mary was free to imagine the outrageous. She pictured the impossible, which led her to the less impossible—finding a way to inspire the Vatican Bank to grant micro loans to the poor. Who knows where that idea will lead? Maybe the micro loan idea won't work, but now she is thinking about what else she might do to make a difference for the people she serves.

Sir Richard Branson, one of the great entrepreneurs of our time and founder of the multifaceted Virgin Brand of companies, didn't start his entrepreneurial life by imagining he would someday fly passengers into space on his Virgin Galactic Airline. He began by dropping out of school and writing about the music business. His Virgin Atlantic Airline got off the ground years later in 1984 with just one plane. It was almost shut down by a nervous banker before it took off on the day of its maiden flight from London to Newark. Branson and his team went on to build the impossible, an international fleet of planes serving passengers on four continents. But he started with the less impossible—one plane—and a commitment to giving passengers a great flying experience.

Life is filled with dreamers who achieved the impossible, yet began by executing the less impossible. The Wright Brothers dreamed of flying above the clouds, but first they had to literally prove they could get their flying machine six feet off the ground.

Henry Ford wanted to build a car that everyone could afford, but first he had to learn how to build an assembly line that would cut costs. He also paid his workers more than the going labor rates, so they could afford to buy the cars they manufactured.

Steve Jobs and his team at Apple dreamed of a music library in the clouds. First they had to convince record companies that it was a good idea to allow consumers to buy their music one song at a time, for ninety-nine cents, when the companies made money selling albums for fifteen times that amount with each purchase. Apple needed other impossible things to occur for them to realize their dream, but they began by achieving the less impossible—transforming an existing MP3 player into the iPod. Before making deals with the record labels, the iPod was just another music player. It took three more years to become the portal to the iTunes music library in the cloud.

All big ideas begin somewhere, and playing God inspires us to dream larger than life before we scale them back to a size that we can manage with available resources. It's what I said I needed to do in the Introduction to this book. Unable to change the world with the sweep of my hand, I decided to start by telling stories that I hoped could ignite a chain reaction of small changes that, when joined, would make a difference. It is like wiring together computer servers until they become a server farm.

Another story in the *Playing God* series illustrates the inverse of imagination and achieving the impossible.

In "Now What's Wrong" (the third story in e-book #4), Harry, the constant complainer, is trapped inside his lifebox. The point of this story is to show how painful life is when we are imprisoned by an irrational fear that the world conspires against us. Harry can't see life from any perspective but from his own paranoid view. His box has no windows or doors. He has no way to escape his box. He demonstrates how miserable life can be without a positive imagination and self-knowledge, which I believe can only be attained when we can see ourselves clearly and objectively.

These stories are supposed to be entertaining and useful. Here is how I suggest putting them to work for you. If necessary, read the stories again and look for ways the characters found answers by escaping their imagined boundaries.

Step out of your own lifebox and take a new look at an old problem that has hounded you. Describe it in writing as if you are God looking at yourself from a distance. Then propose an impossible solution to your problem, one that only God could imagine. Let the idea simmer in your imagination for a few days and feel what happens when your creative power is unleashed. Don't listen to your interior critic. Pay attention to the artist-spirit-creator in you. Your imagination is in there. You have to release it from your lifebox and let it fly free.

You will be amazed by how much more interesting life can be, and how intuitive you become, when you can stand outside your own lifebox and allow yourself to dream.

Thank you for reading my stories. I sincerely hope that they have entertained and inspired you. I'd love to hear if they motivate you to change what needs changing in your life and to appreciate what doesn't.

Please visit Mary Lou and me at our website:

www.DennisandMaryLou.com

Click on the **Contact** button so we can get to know you. I would love to hear your thoughts and questions about the book and about your own life experiences. I promise one of us will personally return your message.

On our website you can see that we specialize in coaching entrepreneurs. We also offer workshops, seminars, and consulting if you are interested in exploring and examining your lifebox and your creative potential. We can show you how to tear down the walls and defeat the fears that hold you back from building the life and the business of your dreams.

Now, go play God.
---Dennis

About The Author

Dennis Edward Green is a husband, father, and grandfather. He is also an award-winning architect, artist, designer, entrepreneur, and best-selling author.

Dennis was raised in Sheridan, Wyoming and attended Idaho State University on a basketball scholarship; he graduated with a BA degree in architecture. After college he became a licensed architect and briefly taught a graduate course in creative thinking called Living Space Awareness at the University of Maryland, College Park. He was a design consultant to the National Endowment for the Arts. He practiced architecture and interior planning for a decade before turning his creative energy to inventing consumer products, writing, and painting.

Together with his wife, Mary Lou, he has invented more than fifty unique consumer products. They built their own sales force and sold their products in more than twenty thousand retail stores in the U.S.A. and around the globe. He has been awarded sixteen patents, more than fifty trademarks, and hundreds of copyrights, for what he calls simple consumer products that solve everyday problems in unique and entertaining ways.

Playing God is his third book. His second book, *The Marriage Story*, is available in hardback only on Amazon.com.

Dennis and Mary Lou are now devoted to teaching and coaching entrepreneurs to grow their businesses.

Learn more about their work here:
http://www.DennisAndMaryLouGreen
http://www.HowToPlayGod.com
Facebook.com/DennisGreenAuthor

www.ingramcontent.com/pod-product-compliance
Lightning Source LLC
Chambersburg PA
CBHW031358160426
42813CB00090B/3157/J